The Story of East Park, Hull

by

Mary Fowler

Highgate of Beverley

Highgate Publications (Beverley) Limited
2002

Aerial view of East Park, 1974.
Photograph by Colin Grant, courtesy of, *Hull Daily Mail.*

British Library Cataloguing in Publication Data.
A catalogue record for this book is available from the British Library.

© 2002 Mary Fowler

Mary Fowler asserts the moral right to be identified as the author of this work.

ISBN 1 902645 27 8

Published by

Highgate of Beverley

Highgate Publications (Beverley) Limited
4 Newbegin, Beverley, HU17 8EG. Telephone (01482) 886017

Printed by Highgate Print Limited
4 Newbegin, Beverley, HU17 8EG. Telephone (01482) 886017

Contents

Bibliography and Acknowledgements iv

The Beginning 1

1887-1918 5

Between the Wars 19

The Second World War 38

'Getting back to normal' 43

Into Modern Times 47

High Hopes 60

Bibliography and Acknowledgements

Much of this book is the result of a long and careful trawl through the minutes of the Parks and Burials Committee (or Parks Committee as its name changed) and of various Sub-Committees, all of which have been named in various parts of the book. I have also studied the plans, deeds, letters, etc. pertaining to East Park in the City Archives and in the Modern Records Office in the Guildhall. Another major source was the *Hull Daily Mail*, from very early in the park's history to the present time, and also other newspapers such as the *Hull Advertiser* and the *Hull Civic News*. Ephemera from various shows in the park were also interesting reading and bolstered the memories of many people by providing exact dates.

Friends and even casual acquaintances have helped, some by the odd sentence that elucidated something I had read but not quite understood. Among these people, Mr. A. Shearsmith and Mr. W. Houlton must be noted. I am grateful, too, for the real interest shown by Mrs. A. Brittain of the *Hull Daily Mail* Library, but, above all, the friendly help of the Hull Local Studies Library staff has been an ever-present encouragement.

Mary Fowler

The Beginning

It could have had a right royal name, as it was opened on the day of Queen Victoria's Golden Jubilee, 21 June 1887. At the ceremony Ald. W. F. Chapman even said that 'East Park' was a misnomer and suggested it be called Victoria Park, but this never happened. It could have been named the Hodge Memorial Park, as it was Ald. Hodge, long a participant in Hull's civic affairs, who had first suggested a park for the eastern part of the town, years before. He lived and worked in East Hull, having a house on Holderness Road at the corner of what became Morrill Street. That, too, could have borne his name, as it had been known as Hodge Avenue, leading down to his oil mill at about the site where the clinic now stands. But, of course, with the economy of expression so common in these parts, East Park is, as often as not, just 'Park' to the people of East Hull.

East Park and West Park were projects of the 1880s at a time when unemployment was high. Hull's first public park, originally called the People's Park, owed its existence in part to the nationwide drives for healthier places for workpeople to live and pass their scanty leisure hours. It was instigated by Zachariah Charles Pearson, whose name began to be used for the People's Park when, nearly twenty years on, official moves were made to establish other parks for the East and West Districts of the rapidly expanding town.

Holderness Road, with a horse-tram route along it as far as the Crown Inn, was the obvious thoroughfare upon which to seek a site for an East District pleasure-ground. At first the parks were the concern of the Property Committee, but an eleven-man Parks (Special) Committee was set up and met for the first time on 12 May 1882. From it, a Sub-Committee of six members, under the chairmanship of the then Mayor, Ald. John Leak, was chosen to deal with the East District. Various sites seemed possible and in August the Sub-Committee looked at:

> 48 acres of Mr. Boswell Jalland's estate at Holderness House, 'beautifully timbered';
> Mr. T. H. West's land, 25 acres where Westcott Street now is;
> 31½ acres of land which had belonged to Mr. J. Lee, offered through his trustees, Messrs. Clarke and Moore;
> the Corporation Farm at Summergangs (38 acres), occupied by a tenant, Mr. Moses Salvidge;
> and lands of Mrs. Ann Watson's Trust: 4 closes or fields, supposed to contain about 46 acres.

All these plots had frontages along Holderness Road, with stream boundaries at right angles to the road and extending back to an open area devoid of housing. The Jalland land was offered at £700 per acre and Lee's land had a number of conditions within the sale description, so eventually the Committee decided to use the Corporation Farm land and buy Ann Watson's closes next to it, further out along the road. The Corporation farmhouse was, in modern terms, at the corner of Summergangs Road. Ann Watson's land began about where the main park gates are now and stretched to the present East Park Avenue. Some of the field divisions were quite substantial ditches and the back boundary was the Lambwath Stream, which was also the town boundary.

After fairly protracted negotiations between the Corporation and Ann Watson's trustees, five closes were bought, covering an area of 38 acres 2 roods 24 perches, at a cost of £16,909. 7s. 6d. Initially, £400 per acre had been offered to the trustees, but the prices paid represented £437. 10s. per acre. Unlike the timbered Jalland estate, this was mostly pasture land with one field of arable. So, with the Corporation farmland, it gave virtually a blank sheet upon which to design a pleasure ground, although at this stage it was intended that 26 acres of the total 76½ acres should be reserved for building sites. These, according to the Borough Accountant's report of 13 February 1883, 'by reason of having roads laid and pavements flagged and being drained and lighted in perpetuity will command a good price for residences of a high class, which, when built, will add to the beauty of the Park'. The Borough Engineer's report of 30 June 1883 specified 24a. 3r. 7p. for building, leaving 52a. 33p. for the park.

Mr. Salvidge, the farm tenant, was given notice to quit once Treasury consent for the purchase of Ann Watson's land was obtained. Having been granted £43. 2s. 6d. in compensation, he moved out on 11 October 1884 and took up the tenancy of another Corporation Farm near the present Southcoates Lane-Preston Road junction. Work soon began on the park layout, but the farm buildings were not demolished and another tenant was installed. There was something not quite straightforward about this interim tenancy. A man called Smith, with two friends, French and

Howlett, took up residence in the house at a rent of 5s. (25p) per week of which Smith paid 2s. (10p) to live in half the house. This he said was an arrangement made with Ald. Chapman of the Sub-Committee. Smith, a Corporation employee from 1 January 1885, was never asked for any rent, but this did not trouble him as he believed he was looking after the place. Later, another man, called Hird, took the other half of the house. Another Corporation employee, who had been a ganger in the laying out of West Park and the new cemetery, Hird was, in June 1888, working in East Park and he, too, regarded the tenancy as part of his wages. Although these irregularities were shown in the minutes of the Parks (Special) Committee in June 1888, it appears that the situation was allowed to continue.

The site of the new park had been described in the Accountant's report in February 1883 in glowing terms: 'easy of access from the town, being close to the terminus of the tram road, and is situated amid very pleasant scenery, having the well-wooded elevation of Sutton in close contiguity on one side and the beautifully timbered grounds of Messrs. Jalland and West on the other. A more picturesque locality of that extent it would be impossible to find on the Eastern side of the Borough or one more adapted to restore the jaded energies of the artisan or man of business when the labours of the day are ended.'

The first sod was cut on 29 October 1884, by the Mayor, Ald. Albert K. Rollitt, using a special spade bought of Messrs. Reynoldson of Queen Street. The first use of the simple name 'East Park' that I have found occurs in the Parks (Special) Committee minutes of 23 December 1885, although West Park, at that time more advanced in construction than East Park, was still referred to as the 'West District Park'. By 1886, with work still continuing, the Borough Engineer was able to report that 140 men were employed at East Park and that the number could rise to over 200. This was good news, as there had been calls for the work on the park to get under way in order to help reduce the level of winter unemployment. About ten of the employed men were paid over 21s. (£1.05) a week; the rest earned up to 18s. (90p) a week.

So the first phase of the park was laid out to a design by Joseph Fox Sharp with a resolution from the Park's (Special) Committee not to exceed the £22,000 estimate. By September, 1886, the project was well advanced, even to the point of granting a Mrs. Allen permission to sell ginger beer in the park, on payment of one shilling (5p) for the season. Tenders were received from firms across the country for various aspects of work and materials. These were: the main roads and drainage, planting, rockery stones, arbours, steps, bridges, urinals, the bandstand and the entrance gates, some of which provided work for local firms, while others were dealt with by more distant specialist companies. For example, a price of £97 from D. Hird of Waterloo Street was accepted for the bandstand, the entrance gates, with large piers costing £235, were to be supplied by the Lion Foundry in Kirkintilloch and rockery stone came from a firm at Dacre Banks near Leeds at 6s. 6d. (32½p) a ton. By the middle of August, 1887, £17,937. 7s. 6d. had been spent and, even after the official opening, timed to coincide with the Golden Jubilee of Queen Victoria, work was still proceeding.

East Park main gates about 1907.

Jubilee Day was marked in Hull by two official openings, that of the covered market in the morning and of the East Park in the afternoon. A commentator on local events, "Verax" in the *Hull Daily Mail*, was quietly scathing about the lack of civic preparation to make the Jubilee a day of rejoicing for all the people of Hull and said the event would be remembered as the 'Jubilee Jumble'. There had been controversy on the matter of payment of banner-carriers in the Trade and Friendly Societies' section of the procession to the park, which had threatened to rob the occasion of some of its splendour. Nevertheless, on 21 June 1887, Jubilee Day, long before two o'clock when the parade was to assemble, large crowds of people had taken up every vantage point in Lowgate, Whitefriargate and other streets where the procession would pass. The Corporation met at the Town Hall (where the Guildhall now is) and the column, headed by the Police Band, set off down Lowgate into Whitefriargate and into Savile Street. (It must be remembered that in 1887 Alfred Gelder Street had not been cut through.) In Savile Street the Trades and Friendly Societies joined in and there was a greater turn-out from these than had been expected after the earlier controversies.

'The Knights of the Golden Horn in their dazzling uniforms took the lead, followed by the Spring Bank Orphan Homes and followed by employees of the Hull Blind Institute on two rullies. These unfortunate men busily employed themselves along the route traversed by the procession by making baskets, an occupation which was looked upon with great interest by the crowd of people who lined the thoroughfare. The Albert Lound Lodge of the local

United Order of Druids and the Peter Cross Whitfield Lodge of Oddfellows, the last-named society carrying aloft a beautiful banner emblematic of the Order, and the Ancient Order of Foresters brought up the rear.' So reported the *Hull Daily Mail*. The importance of the Friendly Societies when there was no State provision in times of sickness and unemployment was very great indeed, and the unexpectedly high attendance of members in the parade may well have been a mark of thankfulness for the extra jobs created during the winter by the construction of the park. The Foresters' section included juvenile members who manned a small flag-bedecked boat on a rully representing the Lifeboat of the Order.

At the park the civic party was accommodated on a temporary platform so that the crowd could see and hear better what was going on. The Rev. J. J. Beddow, vicar of Drypool, offered a prayer and then Ald. Chapman made a short speech, presenting the Mayor, Ald. John Leak, with a walnut and silver-gilt casket enamelled with three crowns, other emblems and pictures of East Park and the Market Hall, commemorative of the day's affairs. The Mayor then declared the park open and the Sheriff, thanking him, remarked upon the physical good such a breathing space as the park would provide for the people of Hull, long into the future. The park as it looked that day was only a beginning, he said. Prophetic words, as East Park would extend greatly beyond its original size in years to come. It was also, the Sheriff said, a memorial in all times as the day in which their beloved Queen completed her half-century of rule over this great and free country. The ceremony closed, as was most fitting on that day, with the National Anthem, played by the Police Band.

East Park was then on the outskirts of the town. There were houses on Holderness Road, but the Garden Village was not yet contemplated and the grounds of Holderness House more extensive than nowadays. Westcott and Lee Streets were not constructed; neither was Summergangs Road, only a track leading past the Corporation Farm buildings to the fields behind. Across the road was the Crown Inn and White House Farm – the area known as Mile House – and, further out still, the mill and cottages where Joseph Rank was born. Beyond the new park's north-eastern side were brickponds, Crescent Villa on the site of another mill, and then, at Ings Road, a little cluster of houses where the toll gate had been. Otherwise, there were flat open fields and hedgerows.

1887-1918

Unlike Pearson Park, when it opened in 1860, East Park did not offer a range of activities such as archery and quoits, but was essentially a central garden area, with fields for cricket and football around it. The main gates on Holderness Road

Called 'the duck pond', this was one of the lakes near the bandstand.
Photograph courtesy of *Hull Daily Mail*.

opened on to a broad carriage drive bordered with chestnut trees, leading to a junction where a loop of road encircling the park's centre came back to its starting point. This was (and still is) the only thoroughfare for vehicles. Strollers could go straight on, along a broad avenue of limes, or take a path across open lawns to a parallel avenue between flower beds and arrive at a south-facing terrace. Beyond the terrace were shrubberies bordering two small lakes joined by a curved waterway between artificial hills covered with trees and shrubs. Between these lakes was the bandstand where various bands performed.

★ ★ ★

Concerts in all the Hull parks were regular and well-attended events in the late Victorian period and by the turn of the century Friday and Saturday evenings were the usual 'band nights'. So popular were they that on 10 July 1901 the Watch Committee received a deputation from the local branch of the Shop Assistants' Union to point out that about 5,000 people were employed in shops, but their places of work did not close until 8 or 8.30 p.m.; some were open until 9.30 p.m. on Fridays and midnight on Saturdays. Thus 'girls of 13 and 14 years never have a chance to hear the music'. The Watch Committee chairman admitted the popularity of the concerts and said there had been 15,000 people in Pearson Park that Friday evening. 'Mother Humber' in the Mail took up the shop assistants' cause, hoping that Thursday would become the regular band night as Thursday was early closing day.

The programmes of music changed little up to the First World War. Starting with a rousing march and including solos so that individual (but unnamed) players could show their expertise, very often a selection of tunes from a favourite show staged at a local theatre was also part of the programme. For example, the two-hour programme of the Hull Borough Police Band on 12 June 1893 was:

Processional March, San Salvatore	F. G. Baker
Valse, Phantome	Gung'l
Gavotte, Eunice	G. Perdue
Overture, Light Cavalry	Suppé
INTERVAL	
Grand Selection, Maritana	V. Wallace
Euphonium Solo, Air Varie	J. Hartmann
Grand Selection, Haddon Hall	Sullivan
Turkish Patrol	T. H. Michaelis

(This piece is intended to illustrate the approach, passing by, and gradual disappearance of a Turkish patrol.)'

At first, the Parks and Recreation Grounds Committee sought bands that would play for no payment, but later a system of tender was introduced. By May 1913, the popularity of the band nights in all the parks was still so high that an advertisement from the Council attracted offers from 17 local bands. Their charges ranged from the £2. 2s. of the Spring Bank Orphanage to the £6 fee of the Salvation Army Icehouse Band. Most bands asked for £5.

There were strict rules governing events in the parks and so, although in 1899 a letter from H. Bailey of 2, Humber Terrace, Ripon Street, asking permission for the Alexandra Brass Band to play in East Park on Thursday evenings received a favourable reply, the request from H. W. Lazenby during the same year, for the First Volunteer Battalion East Yorkshire Regimental Band to play at the bandstand on Sunday afternoon, 29 September, to raise money towards paying off the Infirmary's debts, was granted only if there were to be no public speakers. Earlier in 1889, when the Hull and District Band of Hope League had asked if they could have the exclusive use of either East or West Park for their Annual Demonstration, this was not allowed. Over half a century later this policy was maintained : groups as diverse as the Latter Day Saints and the Conservative Party were refused permission to hold their rallies in the park.

★ ★ ★

Many local football and cricket match results were given in pre-World War One newspapers, but rarely were their venues noted and I have not found one reference to East Park in this connection. However, insight is given, *en passant,* in one of Jupiter Junior's columns of comment in the *Hull Daily Mail,* when he mentions 'a waggonnette with flush-faced raucous-roaring footballers shambling down from East Park'. The Parks Superintendent's report of 25 November 1892 was critical of some

footballers' behaviour, as swearing and bad language used while the games were in progress had been reported to him. When asked to desist, the footballers had taken no notice. It became the Superintendent's duty to report the names of those clubs whose members were heard swearing to the Parks and Recreation Grounds Committee, which had, of course, the power to prohibit them from using the park for their matches. Cricket matches must have been more seemly, for I have not come across any similar comments about players' behaviour.

An early feature of the park was the Model Yacht Pond, a shallow rectangle measuring 390ft. by 130ft. and originally 2ft. 9ins. deep. People spent 'many happy hours sailing their

A long-lasting park amenity: the model yacht pond. Mr. Dennis Green tried out his remote-controlled motor launch, May 1958.
Photograph courtesy of *Hull Daily Mail.*

little craft', according to a one-liner in the *Daily Mail* of 28 June 1893. The East Hull Model Yacht Club had a simple but serviceable Yacht House (20ft. x 15ft.) near the pond and a flagstaff for the club colours. The club held regular tournaments or sailings, the proceedings recorded in the local press with wind strength and direction meticulously included to give quite a nautical flavour to the reports. The tournament of 11 June 1912 was sailed 'in a light northerly breeze, the course being a beat to windward'.

A green was laid out for the popular pastime of bowling in about 1910 and there followed many requests for extra space for the game. It was not until the winter of 1913 when the Distress Committee approached the Parks and Burials Committee for work for the unemployed and offered to pay for the unskilled labour involved that another bowling green was laid out, next to the first one, on the main path leading to the terrace. Bowling and tennis shared the same constraint: there were many clubs wanting to play matches in the park, but to allocate space on a regular basis, especially as many matches were fixed for Thursday (half-day closing) and Saturday, was to deny the general public access at these popular times. Up to 1925 tennis was played on grass behind the nursery area where the Corporation Farm had been. A fairly level piece of ground was selected and the grass mowed much more frequently than the park lawns. Nets were provided and the courts marked out by the park staff, but whether or not they were enclosed with net fences is a moot point, for in 1923 the Parks Superintendent requested that they be netted round, a 'rather costly' job as more than 1,200 yards of netting were needed. I just remember seeing these courts and, judging by that amount of net fencing, there must have been more than I thought.

★ ★ ★

Records of the park's development as seen through Committee minutes are somewhat confusing when the matter of greenhouses is raised, for rarely, if ever, is the word 'conservatory' used to distinguish the glasshouse at the end of the main path below the terrace from those in the nursery area at Summergangs corner. However, a quite definite clue occurs in the minutes of the Parks Committee in November, 1892, after the Committee had inspected a glasshouse recently completed in East Park. This greenhouse, members said, should be opened to the public, a clear indication that here was a conservatory for the display of plants, not a nursery greenhouse. Greenhouses from the estate of Mr. Henry Hodge had been bought for £45 earlier that year and a site in front of the terrace earmarked. There was no greenhouse or conservatory open to the public in East Park previously and it soon became a very popular attraction, as were the glasshouses in the other parks.

The mound, sometimes called Monkey Hill, to the north of the main path leading to the terrace, was built about 1900 as a wind shield for the flower beds and ferns of the display below. It also provided a vantage point in this flat land, especially before the trees were anything like mature.

A childhood delight which continues to please and interest is the aviary. The City Engineer submitted a rough plan for it on 9 April 1913. As it had been provided for in that year's estimates at a cost of about £200, the plan was approved and the work went ahead. A stop for rats was made by cutting a narrow trench round the cage and filling it with concrete; it seems a very simple solution. The overall area of the aviary was 72ft. by 50ft. and, of this, part was wired off for fancy pheasants and similar birds. Occasional gifts of birds were made in later years, especially from Dr. Wildeboer, a near neighbour of the park, in the 1930s.

★ ★ ★

View from the mound, showing Holderness Road and Summergangs Road. How sparse it all looked before the trees matured!
Postcard dated 1911.

MAZE AND FLOWER BEDS, EAST PARK, HULL.

The mound and flower beds.
Postcard dated 1919.

The general public was not so generous with gifts for East Park as towards the other town parks. Some gifts had doubtful value. West Park had even been offered a small alligator by a sea captain and the Committee accepted it, but where it was accommodated, how many small boys it ate, and what became of it is not recorded. Then there was the whale. In 1901, the skeleton of a whale was offered to East Park by the Municipal Museum, but the East Park Sub-Committee recommended that no shelter be provided for it, as the estimated cost was £400-500. The proceedings of the Sub-Committee, reported in the *Hull Daily Mail* under the headline 'Willow, Willow, Whale-y', showed quite clearly that the whale was an embarrassment, even though there had been ideas to stage an exhibition of the whaling industry. As one councillor put it, 'Whales cannot be given away in Hull', so I suppose the whale's skeleton went into the Museum's store. In 1893 Cllr. T. G. Hall had acquired two parts of a pavement from a recently-discovered Roman villa near Lincoln. These fragments were offered to the Parks Committee and, although its Chairman, Ald. John Leak, suggested they be fixed in Pearson Park and East Park, no resolution was taken on the matter, so the mosaics, too, would go into store. I have not attempted to trace their fate, but like to think (and it is just possible) that they are now part of the fine Roman display in the High Street Museums. A model of a full-rigged ship, a gift from Capt. Frederick Lowry, had been received with thanks in October, 1888, but what was done with *that* I cannot say, unless it became part of the Model Yacht Club's property. However, gifts of plants, waterfowl and aviary birds were made very occasionally to East Park, starting with the offer, early in 1885, from E. P. Dixon of Queen Street, of trees to be planted at the time of cutting the first sod of the Parks site. One wonders about the gift of two seagulls from Mrs. James Taylor of Beeton Street in April 1893!

Exchanges between the parks were not uncommon and the three peacocks, seen on a pre-World War One postcard of a grassy area near Khyber Pass, had come from West Park. Khyber Pass was not an official title but one that appears to have been adopted by everyone from the first, as it is even printed in the Council and Committee minutes. (The events on the North-West Frontier, the Anglo-Afghan wars, were still continuing when the park was opened and there was serious activity even as late as 1897.)

★ ★ ★

Major additions were made to East Park in the few years before the Great War through the generosity of T. R. Ferens of Holderness House. At the City Council meeting of 6 April 1911, the Mayor read out a letter from Mr. Ferens, dated 22 March 1911, in which it was noted that the first discussions about the Coronation celebrations had begun. Mr. Ferens then offered his contribution. He had recently bought a strip of land, a field of about 15 acres on Holderness Road, and, on one part with frontage on the road itself, it was Mrs. Ferens' intention 'to erect and endow 12 Alms Houses for aged people'. The rest of the land Mr. Ferens wanted to be made into a playing field for children up to the age of 14 years, and, if the Corporation agreed, he would hand it over to be used in perpetuity for that purpose. 'The gift is in

Khyber Pass with three peacocks in foreground.
Postcard, post-marked 1910.

Beyond the playing field site were the remains of brick-making activities. I cannot say exactly what state this area was in, in 1911, but the kiln had gone, as had the drying sheds, and the diggings were more extensive than when the park opened. There had been sporadic complaints since 1887 about 'burning ballast' when crude firings had taken place, not for bricks or tiles, but to burn clay in clamps to make coarse lumps of brick for ballast or hardcore. Work to turn this industrial site into a playground was well under way in June 1912, for the *Hull Daily Mail*, deploring the fact that boys were swimming in a natural lagoon formed near Alexandra Dock, when this site could have been made into a safe bathing area for £50 to £100 outlay, continued the item with, 'Now something is being done . . .': not to the lagoon but to the brickpond site beyond the King George V Playing Field. The *Mail* reported that a 'huge' brickpond was being converted into an 'immense' swimming bath, its depth varying from 18ins. to 4ft. 6ins. with diving platforms in the middle (4ft. 6ins. near diving platforms seems rather shallow to me. I think they must have been low jetties, perhaps only a few inches above the water surface). The new pond was 60 yds. by 30 yds. in area and thus appears to have covered much of the brickyard behind the playing field, taking in a large brickpond, marked

honour of the Coronation,' the letter continued, and Mr. Ferens suggested that the field might be opened in Coronation week and be named the George V Playing Field or the Coronation Playing Field: 'There is already a road from the park to the field . . .' The motion to accept this generous offer was made by the Mayor, Cllr. T. S. Taylor, himself an East Hull resident and the proprietor of Taylor's Laundry in Southcoates Lane. The offer was accepted unanimously and the name at once decided: the King George V Playing Field. The road referred to was Hawkesbury Street, for already two streets had been cut through from Holderness Road and house-building begun. Hawkesbury Street joined the two new streets at the end away from the main road.

King George V Playing Field from near the boathouse, lake view in the background, 2001.

on a map at the time of its purchase by Mr. Ferens. A simple filter to keep the water from stagnating was yet to be installed and there was an 'immense' sand heap nearby. 'Though the concreting of the pond is not yet completed, hundreds of boys have been enjoying themselves in the water. In a few days it will be handed over.' This was July 1912. Swings and see-saws were bought and the nearby play area soon established, with a large stepped mound, on four sides of which were wooden slides. Next to the playground was the paddling or wading pool intended for girls and younger children. About three acres of land adjoining the bathing pond had been covered with all kinds of plants, chiefly those that grow by water 'and where any who love Nature can wander about at their own sweet will and study their hobby to their heart's content (*Hull Daily Mail*, 5 July 1912)'.

★ ★ ★

On 28 June 1912, Mr. Ferens again wrote to the Corporation,

this time offering land to make a boating lake:

Dear Mr. Mayor,

It has been impressed upon me that, although we have the proud distinction of being the third Port in the Kingdom, we have in connection with our City no boating lake. I have bought a field, containing eight acres, which lies between the East Hull Park and the ponds in connection with the King George V Playing Fields, and it will give me pleasure to have this land dug out to the depth of about 2ft. 6, so that it would be available for boating, and to hand it over to the Corporation for this purpose. The acquisition of this piece of land will join up the East Park and the Recreation Ground, and will provide a further inducement for young people to take their recreation in the open air.

I am,
Very sincerely yours,

T. R. Ferens

The land offered was beyond the new Westminster and East Park Avenues. It went back to the City boundary, the Summergangs Dyke; the open space now opposite Malet Lambert School shows roughly its extent. Work went ahead and a boating lake with islands was constructed in the winter/spring of 1912-13. Mr. Ferens attended the East Park Sub-Committee meeting on 15 March 1913 to give his opinion on what types of boats should be provided. Tenders were sought for single and double sculling skiffs and also for a small motor boat, which, at Mr. Ferens' suggestion, could be used for trips around the lake. Charges for boat hire were fixed at this meeting. The boating lake

Opening of the boating lake by Mr. T. R. Ferens (in light coat, third from left), 8 May 1913. Photograph courtesy of *Hull Daily Mail*.

was opened to the public with a small ceremony in May 1913. By the time of this second gift, £415 had already been spent on the King George V Playing Field in addition to the £500 Mr. Ferens had promised for laying it out.

★ ★ ★

Ferens' gifts of land and their proposed purposes received universal praise, but the gifts of the old watchtower from the Citadel and a part of the old Town Hall tower led to a number of sarcastic letters in the press from members of the public, clearly of the opinion that conservation could go too far. The Citadel, on the east bank of the River Hull at its confluence with the Humber, was originally the creation of Henry VIII in 1541. Its usefulness, of course, dwindled over the centuries; as the government of the country became stable and the Kingdom became United, there was no need for a base for wars against the Scots or the Dutch, nor an arsenal and troops in case the people rose against the monarch. So, in the 1860s the garrison was disbanded and the Citadel pulled down, leaving only fragments here and there. After that, Victoria Dock was excavated, ship-building and ancillary trades began to thrive on the site and the old watchtower, as everyone called it, was built into one of the walls of the Humber Iron Works. When the works' owner, William Bailey, J.P., died, his family decided to donate the tower to the Corporation to enhance one of the public open spaces where it could be seen and appreciated.

The centre of Hull, by then a city, was altered radically in the first decade of the 20th century, a major change being the building of the Guildhall on the site formerly occupied by the Town Hall and various factories. The top of the Town Hall tower, as an old town landmark, was carted off to Pearson Park and re-erected on a mound where it remains to this day. A lower part of the same tower was brought to East Park by Quibell, Sons and Greenwood in the autumn of 1912 at a cost of £3. 18s. (£3.90) because there was no suitable site in Pearson Park. The Sheriff, instigator of the preservation, said this lower stage might be put on the mound in East Park – the mound to the right of the main path leading up to the terrace. However, the stones were merely stored.

Members of the public and the *Mail's* cartoonist made fun of preserving these old artifacts. A cartoon with the caption, 'Imaginary Appearance of our Parks in the near Future', featured the house where murderer Charles Peace slept in Hull; various articles (bottles, pipes, umbrella and, oh horror!, a pair of bloomers) found in the old Town Hall; and a bathtub bearing the notice: 'Robinson Crusoe is said to have sailed from Hull in this'. The legend (fulsome, as was the way at the time) read: 'Several suggestions have been made recently concerning remains of the old Town Hall, etc., which, it is said, should be placed in our parks. Our artist pictures, in the very extreme, what may be the result of these suggestions, which may possibly be followed by others of a less decorous nature.'

So the Town Hall relic remained in store, but the watch tower was put up near the artificial gorge of Khyber Pass and stayed there from 1912 until it was moved to Victoria Dock Village in 1991. The Council plans to seek Heritage Lottery funding for excavation, consolidation and display

The old watchtower in 1991, shortly before removal to Victoria Dock Village.

of the remains of the South Blockhouse at Sammy's Point near The Deep, now (2001) in course of construction. Presumably then, the old watch tower, the south-west Bartizan, can be replaced at or very near its original position.

In August 1887, a letter from a Mr. John Drury had been read in the Parks Committee meeting. Mr. Drury had in his yard three or four old prison doors and pieces of stone and grating which had come from the old Shambles. Since one of the old town gaols had stood at the corner of the street called Butchery until about 1792, upon which a shambles or meat market was established in the early years of the 19th century, it is possible that the relics John Drury was offering to the Corporation for East Park were from that gaol. After all, they would have been stout enough as part of a prison to have lasted all those years. They were accepted and installed in the approach to Khyber Pass. In May 1912, the Parks and Burials Committee decided an iron railing should be put in front of the old prison cells, together with a small plaque giving their history. I cannot trace the plaque; hence my reasoning as to the origin of these relics.

Two stone arches from Newark Castle had been re-erected in the grounds of Holderness House and then given to East Park by Mrs. Jalland about 1900. The stones were not built up again in the park, but numbered and stored with others from the Suffolk Palace in Lowgate. It seems that these must have been used subsequently for rockeries or for edging the lakes because the City Engineer of 1922, Mr. F. W. Bricknell, said he had no idea of their importance. Conservationists may have grieved, but without money enough for the stones' re-erection, there they would have lain – through a war to end all wars which made the mis-placement of a few old stones fade into complete insignificance.

★ ★ ★

A glance through the lists of the park's expenditure shows the expected seasonal bills for water and gas (and after 1911 for the telephone, too), the purchase of coals, of manure and rat poison, of spades and brushes as they wore out, and of seeds and plants. There were occasional repairs, of course, and the saddlery and shoeing needs of the horse which pulled a cart for various purposes. Every so often £1. 10s. (£1.50) or so would be spent on ducks and in May 1913 an item, 'Flamingoes, £7. 10s.', appeared. In committee there was comment about the beauty of the flamingoes in East Park and a suggestion that there should be some in the other parks. Sadly, only a few weeks later, the Parks Superintendent had to report that 'of the flamingoes that were bought, only one is now alive'. After the watchtower was put in the park, Turner and Drinkwater, the high-class photographers, were paid £2. 1s. (£2.05) for taking its picture. Bowls, including some lighter ones suitable for ladies, were purchased of the Asbestos and Rubber Co. In short, the payments made for the upkeep of the park tell the story of its daily round.

★ ★ ★

There was a Parks Superintendent for overall administration of the three parks. Edward Peak was appointed on 25 February 1887 after 25 years as a park gardener, mostly in Pearson Park. His early wage had been 21s. (£1.05) a week, rising by small increments over the years until he was earning 35s. (£1.75) in 1881. When appointed Superintendent, he had five men working under him at Pearson Park, four at West Park, 160 at East Park (that was the time of planting out the new park) and 44 at the Cemetery. The Borough Engineer's Staff Committee which appointed him was unanimous in declaring that the salary of £130 and a house were 'wholly inadequate for the many valuable services which he renders to the Corporation'. He was granted leave with expenses from time to time to visit, for example, the R.H.S. show at Chelsea and the great horticultural show in Ghent, and in 1889 was granted a fortnight's holiday to enable him to take a sea voyage for the benefit of his health.

A Park Keeper's lodge was provided for in the early stage of planning East Park; the Borough Engineer's report of 30 June 1883 designated a lodge at the main entrance, but this was not built. A plan of 1903 exists and the lodge is marked on the 1908 O.S. map, so it must have been built between those dates. There was to be another lodge for the park gardener where an area was reserved for a nursery garden, glasshouses and stabling on the site of the old Corporation Farm.

Some park staff were provided with uniforms, at first from Edwin Davis's store in the Market Place. In 1891, to take a year at random, the East Park foreman was F. Judson and the Park Keeper H. Anderson. Both had uniforms; Mr. Judson earned 30s. a week for being in charge of the day-to-day running of the park; Mr. Anderson earned 21s. plus a house,

Park-keeper's uniform, including beard and stick! 1901.

while Mr. G. Bird, the horseman, also uniformed, earned 21s. and had a house to live in. There were also five labourers on the payroll at that time. Revenue came into the park through the hire of bowls and, later, boats, band payments and sometimes in a way we should not think of today. Part of the ground was kept for hay, not only for the horse, but in a good year for profit. In the spring of 1892 a man from Nornabell Street bought that year's surplus of 8-9 tons for £25. 10s.

★ ★ ★

So the life of the park went on. The bands, the fountains in the two small lakes and the children all played in their own way. The footballers, cricketers, bowls players, rowers and those who merely walked or sat in the park to enjoy the air

Enjoying a walk in the rockery. Date about 1910.

17

and the passing scene used the park frequently and, for the most part, with respect. However, little incidents sometimes marred this idyllic picture. Reports of obscene language, of theft and damage to property reached the police or the Parks Committee. Notices forbidding the use of obscene language were posted; the police investigated the theft of ducks and duck eggs; and in 1912, a Mrs. Leslie and a Mr. Hall had to appear before the Committee with their respective sons who had damaged a park seat. The boys were severely reprimanded by the Chairman; they expressed regret and promised not to do it again. Because there had been objectionable characters hanging about on the path beside the Ferens' Almshouses at the approach to the King George V Playing Field, a gate was put across and an attendant appointed to patrol the area where the children played. As for behaviour on band nights, when the thousands who thronged the park were mostly young people, the general standard was good, but as the *Mail* observer put it pithily – there was 'a bit of larking on the outskirts'.

In fact, at the outbreak of World War One the life of the park was fairly bouncing along. A great extension to the boating lake, again financed by Mr. Ferens, but not as an outright gift this time,

The boating lake's first extension went nearly as far as the yacht pond.
Photograph, September 2001.

was under construction. It was excavated on Corporation land except for about two acres (on what is now the James Reckitt Avenue side) which had to be bought of a neighbouring landowner, a Mr. May, in order to divert the course of the Lambwath Stream and ensure that the narrowest part of the new water was wide enough to be safe for rowing boats. The various park activities were popular; problems, seen from the

vantage point of the 21st century, seem minimal, and the imminent cataclysm did not overshadow any of the buoyant plans for the park. When an officer of the local military asked in February 1913 for recruiting poster boards to be put up at East Park gates, the reply was that the Committee was willing to allow a case to be fixed for all regimental notices, but could not see its way to allow further notices to be fixed about the park entrance.

★ ★ ★

A sombre change comes over the minutes of the Parks and Burials Committee by 1915-16. There are far more acts of damage and lawlessness, staff is depleted, not only by men being in the services, but by a much increased sick-list at all seasons.

Economies were urged and practised and, although great effort was made to retain the park and its activities as it had been, it was just not possible. Nevertheless, the extension to the boating lake was accomplished by the middle of November 1915, despite Ald. Richard Gillett's jibe in 1914 that they were going on with 'this blessed lake' until it got to Sutton. In fact the extension brought the end of the lake nearly to the Yacht Pond. It had cost £2,257. 11s. 7d, somewhat less than the £2,500 estimate. On reading of the proposed extension in the *Eastern Morning News*, Mr. Ferens had promptly offered a loan for the work, so pleased was he with the lake's popularity. The City Engineer had said in February 1914 that the extra area would accommodate another five or six rowing boats and another motor boat, probably sufficient to pay for the work in a season.

But the future was to be much different from those golden days up to August 1914.

Between the Wars

To look at the years between the wars is to look at an expanding city. A horse tramway as far as Lee Street served well enough in 1887, but by the outbreak of war in 1914 a great number of houses had been built and were a-building on new streets off Holderness Road. Westcott and Lee Streets were assuming their present form, Summergangs Road was cut through and eventually made a link to Sutton. Telford, Brindley and Faraday Streets had good family homes for people who could afford to move out from smaller houses in streets and terraces nearer the town.

The long line of family houses on Holderness Road stretched to the new Aberdeen and Portobello Streets, with gaps only for Rank's mill, the Baptist church and some shops. The electric tramway was inaugurated in April 1900 and the tramsheds with an elaborate terracotta frontage completed in 1903. Even before the change of the City boundary in 1929 to Ganstead Lane or thereabouts, the tram route was extended (September 1925) as far as Ings Road, where the terminus remained until the departure of the trolley buses from Hull's transport system after World War Two. So, what with more houses and an improved tram service, East Park had a great number of potential visitors from east of the river and beyond. An indication of the park's popularity is seen in the number of people using facilities for which a charge was made. For example, in the 1919 season, 18,471 people paid 1d. each to play bowls.

The boating lake was still very much used, but in March 1918 the motor boat had to be taken out of service as by

19

then petrol substitute and gas were prohibited for pleasure boats. The City Engineer asked for a special permit but was refused, and the minutes of the Parks and Burials Committee reflect the members' sadness that the motor boat trips must be discontinued as they knew how many thousands of children had derived pleasure from them. At the end of the war, the rowing boats were showing signs of wear and, although as a stop-gap some second-hand boats had been bought from Bridlington, many people refused to use them. Of even more concern, was the fact that the lake itself was leaking very seriously, 24 leaks having been identified. A concrete apron or screen wall abutting the lake on the Lambwath Stream side was needed, work to be carried out in the winter of 1919.

1919 was a dour year. Many staff were ill as the influenza epidemic raged across the country, and deficiencies due to wartime neglect came to light while people struggled to return to peacetime living. Changes elsewhere affected the park; for example, the East Riding Football Association had to seek additional grounds, as many of their pitches had become wartime allotments. With 3,500 local players, the Association needed land for 50 clubs to practise and play their matches. Fourteen acres were assigned to football clubs in East Park and this allowed for nine pitches; there were also two smaller pitches for boys under 14 years on the King George V Playing Field. On some Saturdays, seven or eight clubs had to be refused. Dressing-room facilities were also requested and negotiations were in hand in 1919, for the purchase of old army huts to fill this need.

★ ★ ★

On 9 April 1919, the Committee discussed the best site for a tank to be presented to the City through the National War Savings Committee. It was placed near the bandstand, but in 1921 was moved to a position nearer to the park entrance. It eventually came to rest near Khyber Pass, where many older people remember it. In late 1919 the City Engineer took delivery of four Howitzers and a field gun which were stored in the various parks. Again, this evokes memories for older people, for a gun accompanied the tank as one of the 'attractions' of Khyber Pass: not a case of beating swords into ploughshares, but of leaving these instruments of war in view as a reminder of its horror and, in contrast, as playthings for children too young to realise their awesome import. The tank ceased to be of interest to the general public (according to the Superintendent) and was sold for £77. 10s. to the highest bidder, Thos. W. Ward of Sheffield, in April 1937.

★ ★ ★

The immediate post-war years were not all doom and gloom, however. The band concerts, so far fairly stereotyped in form, were loosening up to include different types of popular music, and the idea of a dancing floor as a ring around the bandstand was mooted. This was slow in coming to reality. In the spring of 1920 the legal opinion was that, although the Corporation could provide swings and other articles of recreation and charge for their use, it was not clear if a dancing floor was such an 'article of recreation'. Further, although the Corporation had the power to set aside parts of the park for specific games such as football and cricket, it did not seem that dancing was a game. The outcome was that, if the Corporation provided a floor, it could not be fenced and therefore the public would be allowed free access. A music and dancing licence was needed, nonetheless. By 10 January 1923, Cllr. Archibald Stark, with Mr. Witty, the Parks Superintendent, had been to Woodhouse Moor, Leeds, and also to Wortley and Armley near Leeds to inspect dancing floors in their parks. Neither Armley's ('of asphalt, very rough and destructive to boots') nor Wortley's ('concrete, better than Armley but not very smooth') had in the first instance been laid as dancing floors but they had been used without any special preparation – and without complaint. No charge was made for dancing, but a collection, usually amounting to £12 or £16 (or up to £60 if a special band were playing) was taken at the gate. It was left to Hull's City Engineer to find out the comparative costs of different types of flooring, including wood and mosaic, for a dancing floor for East Park. Subject to being allowed to borrow the £2,353 needed for concrete or some similar hard material, the provision of the dancing floor was listed in the 1923-4 estimates, but in December 1923 was postponed for a further year. It was not until June 1925 that the Parks Committee passed a resolution that work should begin on a 41ft.-wide asphalted area round the bandstand. Since it would cost less than previous dancing floor quotations and, at £584, no loan was needed, the cost became part of a supplementary estimate for that year. So, apparently, the matter was resolved : no wood, no mosaic. Many people who remember dancing round the bandstand in the thirties have told me that they danced on asphalt and enjoyment outweighed the crudity of the surface.

* * *

A major move to develop the park still further came in a proposal from Cllr. Stark in 1922 that the boating lake, extended south-westwards as the war began, be now extended in the other direction towards Ings Road. Much of the land required for this belonged to the Leonard Chamberlain Charity and there was also need to acquire a small area at the far northern corner from Mr. Finch who was building houses on Ings Road opposite another brick-works (where Ings School now is). The shape of the total parcel of land was irregular, from the King George V Playing Field, behind the building plots which became Lake View and Lake Drive, and behind the old Willows brickpond. Access and main road frontage came later.

The Sculcoates Union had a large number of men on relief, 1,600 of them able-bodied. The Workhouse authorities suggested that as many as possible of these men be taken on by the Corporation, who would not have to pay wages as the Board of Guardians would provide relief payments. This idea was adopted via the Parks Committee. Through May into June 1923, the average weekly workforce from the Sculcoates Guardians was 395 and good progress was made.

Many of the old rowing boats had been sold off as unfit for use. A Boats Sub-Committee had been formed and its Chairman, Cllr. Stark, together with the Deputy City Engineer, went to London to view the situation in Regent's Park, a visit suggested by Mr. Ferens. He wanted them to see some novel boats used by children there. They also saw boating ponds at Clapham Common and Epping Forest, noting that there were always boats on the water and a boatman in attendance whenever children were there. Cllr.

Stark and the Deputy Engineer felt that the children's boats were inapproprate craft for the main lake in East Park and proposed that a boating lake for children under 12 years be constructed. Hence the Peter Pan Lake behind Lake Drive, an oval pond with sloping sides and an island in the middle, which was opened on the same day as the boating lake extension, 26 July 1924.

With the alteration to the main boating lake came alterations to the swimming and paddling pools for children. A new swimming pond, for girls this time, was constructed by the Sculcoates Guardians workforce, so that the only expense for labour incurred by the Corporation was the making of lattice-work dressing cubicles, but the total expenditure exceeded the sanctioned loan by a wide margin as the girls' pool and the Peter Pan Lake had not been accounted for in the application. Further loans were necessary. A paddling pool was made on the south side of the boating lake extension; there had been a pool there before, of course, but here was the large round shallow pond near the park bridge, remembered by many East Hull people of an older generation. The bridge, too, was part of the new works and was roughly the boundary line between the original Ferens' Boating Lake and its final extension.

Access to and from Holderness Road, necessary now that the park had extended so far, led to the purchase of land belonging to the Tower Grange estate. At first only a route from the park to the main road was envisaged, but when the deputation (Dr. G. W. Lilley, Cllrs. Thomas Carrick and A. Stark) saw the property and began negotiations with the owners, Messrs Wm. Jackson & Son Ltd., they reported to the Committee that, as there was no other property or plot of land that would give frontage on to Holderness Road and since the Jackson estate contained a large number of well-built greenhouses with special heating apparatus, they considered the inclusive price of £3,250 a worth-while investment. Most of the greenhouses could remain, they said, and two could be taken to other parks. The area would provide a convenient entrance to the park for the growing population of that part of the City.

★ ★ ★

I do not think the provision of refreshments in the park was ever very satisfactory. At first it was the concern of a tenant of a small refreshment pavilion near the bandstand. The tenancy was renewed annually with several incumbents over the years up to World War One; some of them were not very satisfied with the situation. Comments about the service voiced in Committee were niggles rather than outright complaints until June 1912, when Dr. Lilley said he had taken a lady to East Park on band night and was unable to provide her with refreshment. 'The arrangements for the canteen in East Park are somewhat crude and out of date. We ought to have a proper pavilion with a verandah and tables outside,' he said, adding that as three to four thousand people were in the park on band nights, it was 'odd' that the accommodation was not more inviting. Sweets and confectionery were obtainable at the pavilion. There was neither gas nor electricity, so it would have been difficult to make tea. Certainly there was no alcohol, but mineral waters were most likely on sale, as Hindle's and other manufacturers were well established in Hull. After Dr. Lilley's comments,

a report was invited on catering in all the parks and someone suggested that an outside firm such as Field's be brought in. Field's was a high-class grocery with two cafés in Hull and others elsewhere in Yorkshire. Mr. Winsall, the East Park caterer at this time, took the tenancy again the following year, but complained that the Refreshment Pavilion was unsuitable both in site and accommodation and asked if a better pavilion in a more convenient position could be erected. Brought to Committee, this request was deferred on 8 July 1913, even though members said that the caterer did his best under the circumstances. Not long after, the war intervened.

When the war was over, there were years of plans and deferments and the evidence from Committee minutes and extant plans (some undated) in the City Archives makes the progress, if any, of the story difficult to follow. In February 1922, the Town Clerk applied to the Unemployment Grants Committee for a grant for a boathouse. An initial rebuff was followed in a few weeks by the UGC approving the new works on condition that preference was given to ex-servicemen workers. To obtain the grant, the Corporation had to pay wages below the Union rate, but, even so, in April the work was begun, the City Engineer being of the opinion that the new boathouse could be used as a refreshment room in the current year, with adaptations such as the addition of counters to the tune of about £50. In June came a complaint from the Branch Secretary of the National Federation of Building Trades Operatives because bricklayers at the boathouse were being served by other than builders' labourers. Building wages were lowered from 1 June 1922, craftsmen earning 1s. 8d. per hour (about 9p) and labourers 1s. 3d. (about 6p) an hour. This was one of the first signs of tightening regulations on labour which ultimately led to the General Strike of 1926.

The new boathouse was at the end of the lakeside path straight on from East Park Avenue, at the corner where the first boating lake extension began. Part was used as a Refreshment Pavilion after its completion in early August 1922; the tenant caterer was Mr. F. E. Wells. This café was quite separate from the old Refreshment Pavilion, which continued until completely destroyed by fire on 4 September 1925. Then in November 1922, Mr. Bricknell, the City Engineer, produced a plan for a new pavilion and roof garden to cost £2,140, for which provision was to be made in the next year's estimates.

Tea gardens had been laid out near the boathouse and a band played there during the afternoons of that year's Gala and Regatta. Again, in October 1925, plans for 'a new refreshment pavilion etc., and boathouse, the boathouse of which has already been erected' were submitted to the Parks Committee. This undated plan is identifiable in the Archives as the corresponding minute is appended showing that Mr. Ashley Cooper was the Quantity Surveyor. Meanwhile, the boathouse, with a new concrete floor, was to be used as a refreshment room the following season. No reference to the building of a complete pavilion and roof garden is made in the minutes, but a glimpse is given of the primitive conditions at the boathouse café in April 1927, in a suggestion from the City Engineer that a pail closet should be fixed at the rear of the building, rendered unobtrusive by ricker fencing, for the use of the personnel of the café. It was not until 1929 that the Municipal Restaurant Committee recommended the installation of gas and electricity at the boathouse and also said how much a verandah would enhance its value as a café.

In my childhood in the 1930s, I do not remember any provision for refreshments in the park, but friends tell me that they were obtainable at the boathouse. The 'cinema architecture' elevations of planned buildings that I have seen recently in the City Archives, showing a rounded forecourt and steps leading to a fenced roof garden, stir no memories whatsoever. However, I have an image, be it from true memory or from an imaginative invention I cannot say, of the plot in front of the boathouse divided into areas with ricker-work poles supporting small pink climbing roses. Perhaps this was the tea garden.

Meanwhile, from their first building before the 1914-18 war, shops at the corners of East Park and Westminster Avenues with Hawkesbury Street did a roaring trade in sweets and ice-cream; in two of them were little tea-rooms. Many people will also recall the tiled tables in the café at the rear of Mr. Butnick's shop at the top of East Park Avenue on Holderness Road. The Parks Committee resisted many requests for ice-cream and other stalls in the park over the years, and I think the position of the boathouse café was a curious and out-of-the-way site for a café anyway.

Perhaps Dr. Lilley was more sophisticated than most people who went to the park. The young people dancing round the bandstand had little money to spare and the thousands of children who played in the park were more

all Hull parks. Tenders of W. H. Gaze and Sons, Ltd. of Kingston-on-Thames at £466. 11s. 4d for six courts behind the East Park Avenue houses and of the Permanent Hard Court Co. Ltd. of London at £455 for six courts behind the Willows pond, were accepted. Fewer people wanted to play on grass, but eight courts remained in use at least up to 1939. I suppose the demand for hard courts came as more and more people saw the game played on the cinema screen or heard about it on the wireless, and so, even at amateur level, it was changing from gentle pat-ball to a harder, faster game of skill and precision. Not that all the participants who paid 3d an hour for doubles or 4d an hour for singles use of the court could provide the interested spectators (and there were usually people watching) with displays of skill, speed and sustained rallies, as many of the players were just learning the game. The original hard surface was brick dust, but, in 1931, the newly-appointed Parks Superintendent, Mr. J. E. Roberts,

likely to come with a bread-and-butter sandwich and water in a screw-cap Camp coffee bottle than with money to spend on refreshments. Ha'penny for an ice-cream cornet, yes, but there were tight limits in East Hull in the 1930s. In those days, too, the Council's Economy (Special) Committee cast its shadow over many projects, as its aim was to keep the City's spending within bounds. The boathouse café with roof garden was never built.

* * *

After a deputation had visited Glasgow in the autumn of 1924 to see how many hard tennis courts, putting greens and bowling greens were in that city, in January 1925, the Parks Committee decided to provide hard tennis courts in suggested a proprietary material called 'Griselda' should be used because the first surfacing was by then in a bad state.

The bowls players were not quite so fortunate. Plenty of requests for more greens had reached the Committee, but nothing was done until late 1930, when ground was levelled at the back of the park lodge ready for turf. That December, turf was in short supply, but a member of the City Engineer's department had been to Lancaster and the west coast to make a selection of sea-washed turf, samples of which were shown to the Committee. The first firm commissioned to prepare the greens withdrew its tender, and in December 1930 another firm was called in. This was Henry Hill & Co., Hull. The start of laying the turf was thus delayed and it was not finished until the middle of May, whereupon the Parks Superintendent said the new greens should not be used in the 1931 season 'on account of the extra nursing which would be required'.

So the new Cumberland turf greens were not opened until March 1932 and the players, charged 3d. a game here, were obliged to wear overshoes (1d. per game) to protect the special turf. The value of wearing overshoes was noted at the end of the season. There followed several years of regular requests from the East Park Veterans' and Bowling Club for better accommodation at the old greens and a Parks deputation even went to see how things were in Greenhill Park, Huddersfield, before (a year later, in January 1935) viewing East Park. In October 1935, a shed at the entrance to the King George V Playing Field was considered, but it needed £100 to provide the accommodation the Bowling Club required and therefore the matter was deferred until 1936. Meanwhile, the shed received £10-worth of repairs and presumably was moved to the bowling green.

The Cumberland turf greens, both in East Park and at Springhead, won prizes and commendations in the annual competition held by the *Yorkshire Evening Post*. Prize money was small, but the results brought the work of the parks staff to wider notice. In July 1939, a plan for a bowls pavilion was accepted by the Parks Committee, but, once again, a war intervened.

During the twenties and thirties there were also rather half-hearted attempts to add putting greens to the amenities of the park, the first resolution to that effect being proposed on 8 October 1924. A triangular plot between the tennis courts and the Peter Pan Lake was converted into a little putting green and was, I think, intended for children. Even more vague in my memory was another green which existed near the older bowling greens. Equipment was bought in the spring of 1925 and the charges fixed at 2d. per person per game of 18 holes, including the use of putter and ball. By July, the putting greens were 'being freely used by the public', and for the first season the receipts were £52. 15s. (which represented 330 games) against expenditure of £21. 2s. 4d. When improvements were made to the original bowling greens in the spring of 1934, the nearby putting green was dispensed with and the ground levelled 'so that children may use it for a playground'. The next summer, the use of putting greens was discontinued in all the parks, with the exception of the one near the Peter Pan Lake. I think that remained until the outbreak of World War Two.

* * *

The splash boat's tower in June 2001.

*Splash! The young and not so young enjoy
the splash boat together.*
Photograph courtesy of *Hull Daily Mail.*

One of the long-lasting joys for young visitors to the park was, and still is, the splash boat or water chute. The first mention of it came in 1927 when the City Engineer submitted plans to the Boating and Open Spaces Sub-Committee. Particulars of chutes from different firms were called for, and at the Parks and Burials Committee meeting of 9 January 1929 it was decided that a water chute should be erected. The patentees were Messrs. Chas. Wicksteed & Co. Ltd., and £1,400 was borrowed for the apparatus. The tower housing was built by the City Engineer's Department as they had offered the lowest tender at £474. 12s. 5d.

The run started 22 feet above water level. For a penny the child climbed the steps to the top of the tower and then was let down the slope in the boat, which held perhaps a dozen, for nearly 100 feet And then, Splash!, into the lake for a horizontal run of 78 feet. I must be the only long-time East Hull resident who has never been in the splash boat. One could see little boys with plenty of coppers going on it time and time again. The rumble of the boat being winched back up and, more especially, the noise as it careers down the slope, the screams and splash can be heard for some distance, despite the muffling effect of intervening trees. Children still go on it and it is therefore one instance of the simple, straightforwardly mechanical device beating more modern playthings hands down.

* * *

In May 1918, a letter was received from the Secretary of the Fresh Water Fish Committee of the Board of Agriculture and Fisheries regarding the capture of eels and the re-stocking with elvers of any enclosed waters under their control. I think that, when the children's play-ground was made, there must have been another brickpond, or part of the large one from which the paddling place was fashioned, which remained in or near its native state, because, following the letter, the Parks Superintendent was authorised to buy 2,000 elvers 'for the brick pond' at King George V Playing Field. The cost was six shillings (30p). There must have been a separate pond remaining, for, although the paddling pond and the boys' swimming pond had used old brickponds in their construction, I cannot think that a large quantity of elvers would have been introduced into either, even during a war when food was scarce. A later offer of elvers, in April 1920, was refused.

Although I have found no mention of stocking it with fish when it was opened, the Ferens Boating Lake was the venue for angling matches in the 1920s, with the schoolboys' match an annual event. Then, in January 1929, a catch of 13,000 good roach, netted by the Hull and District Amalgamated Anglers' Association, from the old Stoneferry Waterworks reservoirs, was transferred to the boating lake. Fish from the ornamental lake near the bandstand, originally stocked in 1891, were transferred to the boating lake in the early part of 1933 by personnel of the Market Weighton Canal Co. for a payment of £10.

In 1924 seven fine swans were sent to Hull by His Majesty's Swan Keeper. Some went to Pearson Park, the rest to East Park, enough to make up the stock in both parks. There were regular annual regattas on the lake, for which admission to the park was charged, and there was always a

The boating lake, early days 'Older persons seem to be crowded out'.
Postcard, 1913.

Swans being fed near the splash boat.
Photograph courtesy of *Hull Daily Mail*.

range of boats to exercise different types of rowing skill. The lake was enjoyed by many; a picture of 1913 shows a tight queue of lads and young men waiting at the ticket office. In fact, in those early days, young people were so eager to go boating that it was said in one Committee meeting, 'Older persons seem to be crowded out.' Scenes like this led to different arrangements at ticket office and landing stage, but the popularity of the boats continued and perhaps, without those pushing queues of eager young men, the proposals to extend the lake would never have been made.

A later spectacle on the lake which I always remember, had no connection with boats. In one of those dreadful winters of the early 1940s during the war, the lake froze so hard that hundreds of people walked and slithered and skated on the ice. We pupils from Malet Lambert ignored the bridge and walked, hundreds of us, straight across from school to the end of Westminster Avenue. Those who didn't normally go home that way detoured. And it lasted for weeks. One Sunday, my mother wished to see the frozen lake and we went through the Tower Grange entrance. There was no Clean Air Act then and the big freeze came

under heavy grey skies polluted with smoke, yet in East Park were scenes worthy of a Breughel or an Avercamp. I was amazed to see how many people had skates and were quite proficient on them. A middle-aged neighbour, an office worker, whose sole hobby (I thought) was growing roses, was skating among the crowd, skilfully avoiding people and

The frozen lake, a view near the site of the old boat-house. The once-elegant bridge marks roughly the extent of the original lake, with the second extension beyond.
Photograph courtesy of *Hull Daily Mail*.

thoroughly enjoying himself. Most people had come out of curiosity, as we had, but left with a memory such as mine.

In 1924, the park had been kept open until 10 p.m. to allow opportunity for skating. It must have been at a time of the full moon, for there were no other lights. Further back, before the boating lake was thought of, there were winters when the ornamental ponds had frozen. Consideration was given to charging people for skating, but fortunately not implemented. Notices were put up when the park staff saw that the ice was thick enough and warnings not to break the ice were also displayed. Of course the waterfowl were protected; an area of water near the island opposite Malet Lambert was kept clear of ice during the wartime winter and the ducks, geese and swans were confined to it for weeks.

★ ★ ★

Following correspondence between the Lord Mayor, Frank Finn, and the Secretary of the East African Group Committee of the 1925 British Empire Exhibition, the City was offered a carved Arab doorway which had framed the entrance to the East African Pavilion and was a copy of a doorway in Zanzibar. The Town Clerk made transport arrangements, but discussion on the place where the doorway was to be used and exhibited in Hull was deferred.

The Town Clerk had, the previous year, been offered a Chinese sampan for a mere £10 as it stood at another Wembley exhibition. Being 25 feet long, of 8 feet 6 inches

The Arab doorway in Khyber Pass.
A picture of the early 1930s. Photograph courtesy of *Hull Daily Mail.*

beam and with a draught of 18 inches, it would have presented a bizarre sight on the Ferens Boating Lake. £12 would have transported it to a Hull goods station, but the Committee would not entertain the offer. However, the Arab doorway came to Hull and was stored. Not until the summer of 1930 did the Parks and Burials Committee do anything about it, when, on 1 July that year, they decided it should be erected at the entrance to Khyber Pass. There was a path along the top of the high ground forming the cliffs of the artificial gorge and a bridge over Khyber Pass itself. The gates were fitted under the bridge and formed yet another rather strange artifact to be seen in that vicinity.

★ ★ ★

More important than Arab doorways or Chinese sampans was a great improvement made to the park's amenities by the building of a substantial set of ladies' and gentlemen's toilets near the main entrance in 1927, in time for the 1928 O.S. map. Some lavatories in the park rarely seemed to be in a good, clean condition, but the ones at the entrance were kept quite clean and had attendants. Sited as they were, they seemed to be more a part of Holderness Road than of the park itself, but at a time when people walked long distances, even to the town and back from the outskirts, they were an important amenity.

★ ★ ★

In 1928, Messrs King & Co. Ltd. gave two demonstrations of their broadcasting apparatus to provide music for dancing in East Park and followed this with three evening concerts by the same method, at an inclusive cost to the Corporation of £6. There were still plenty of bands in the locality wanting to perform in the park, but in May 1929 Messrs B. Cooke & Son, Hull, supplied an Igranophone complete with four moving coil loudspeakers and an Igranic microphone control unit at £230 for amplifying music. It is interesting to note that the ironmongers and scientific instrument makers were first on the scene with the new technology. In the summer of 1929, charges for the band concerts were adults 6d. or 3d. depending on whether the listener was in the inner or outer area around the bandstand; children paid 2d. However, the bands did not play *al fresco* in the winter months and so gramophone recitals were given instead, using the new equipment. The Igranophone was used for a dancing concert on Easter Monday, 1930, and this form of music was often used thereafter. It posed problems of overtime for park staff and, as the Parks Superintendent said, 'Undoubtedly extra attention is needed and it is certain that, if the principle of time off for time worked is conceded, the maintenance of the park will suffer.' There had been 43 Igranophone concerts in 1929, presumably including some in the autumn and winter, and 300 hours had been worked by the park staff in this connection, the equivalent of one man's work for six weeks. Unfortunately, the man most skilled in operating the new equipment, a Mr. Marshall, was one of the key men in the glasshouses. He was awarded overtime payments, but the rest of the staff involved had their rosters changed to accommodate this new aspect of their work, without receiving overtime pay. Bands continued to play in the park, both for dancing and for concerts, but the era of piped music had arrived.

★ ★ ★

Between the wars, with the major trees of the main avenue and the encircling roadway becoming so mature that they were thinned out from time to time, and with the smaller prunus, silver birch and shrubs having grown and thickened so as to form a screen at the back of the terrace, the setting for colourful flower beds in a more open space showed the foresight of the early planners. The flower gardens in the centre of the original park were always a joy to behold, and the shapes and colours of the bedding plots, changed as they were each season, provided over years of regular visits a kaleidoscope of shifting hues. With trees maturing as a backdrop, East Park came to its peak in the late 1930s. At one side of the path leading up to the conservatory, the flower beds were backed by the mound with a kind of maze built around it, and behind the mound, winding paths led through the rock gardens to the grotto under the bridge carrying the path leading to the aviary.

The park gardeners produced new varieties of plants and showed them in the flower beds, just as we see the latest strains on television programmes today, the colours and arrangements giving ideas to amateur gardeners. In the 1930s, the forerunner of all today's gardening programmes was Mr. Middleton's weekly talk on the wireless and public gardens often provided the illustration. Sometimes entirely new plants were produced in the park nurseries. For example, in 1901, Mr. Judson, the East Park gardener, produced 'a new species of chrysanthemum', which the Parks Superintendent described as a rare event so far north as the seeds were difficult to set. An application to market the new plant met with a mixed reception in committee, Dr. Holder

supporting the idea and applauding Mr. Judson's 'high character' research, while Ald. Gillett said it would be a dangerous precedent to allow the gardeners to trade. The vote was in Mr. Judson's favour; he was permitted to sell his chrysanthemum provided that specimens remained in East Park. Then, in the early 1930s, the gardeners at Tower Grange were successful in raising a new type of calceolaria, a cross between the herbaceous form and *Calceolaria Banksii*. I do not think it was sold, but it was given wider public display than the park beds by being exhibited at a flower show in York. I first saw calceolarias in East Park and learned the name, along with the names of many other plants not then common in suburban gardens. The park, therefore, was a place of research and education as well as beauty and relaxation.

★ ★ ★

There must have been a floral clock in East Park (and Pearson Park, too) by 1911, as there are recorded payments for the hire of floral clock parts in November of that year. However, the East Park clock may have fallen into disuse and possibly been dismantled, perhaps about the time of the First World War. Certainly I remember the great anticipation before King George VI's Coronation in 1937 when a floral clock was to be planted and in use, to the left of the avenue leading up to the conservatory. However, the makers, Potts of Leeds, could not have the clock (and another for Pearson Park) ready for that season because of a difficulty in obtaining raw materials. The concrete chambers for both clocks had been constructed at a cost of about £55, but, it

miraculous thing to me as a young child, and, as far as I recall, it kept good time. The clock was a major point of interest in the park until the 1970s.

★ ★ ★

There had been summer galas in the park throughout the twenties, and by the late thirties a tradition of large-scale entertainment in East Park had become established. The two major events of the decade, George V's Silver Jubilee in 1935 and George VI's Coronation two years later, gave ample reason for celebration, and, although East Park was not the only venue, it was the largest site in the City and able to accommodate thousands of people. The East Park Gala during Civic Week in October 1933 attracted more than 200,000 visitors over the week and evoked the following comment from the *Hull Daily Mail:* 'It is not easy to arrange a competent entertainment in such a large park as East Park,

appeared that they might have to be dismantled if the clocks were not forthcoming. The Coronation (Special) Committee was to pay for the clocks, but if they did not arrive within the current year, there might be no money available for their purchase. The cost was £400 for the two. They were not installed in time for the Coronation, but anticipation turned to joy when they were in position, and many people came on purpose to see East Park's new attraction. It was quite a but the Parks Committee has gained much knowledge of such events in Hull Parks for the future.' The Air Ministry authorised a fly-past of No. 35 Bomber Squadron and a long procession of decorated floats travelled from Ferensway to the park, where, during the week, a programme offered concerts, variety shows, a fire-fighting display, a motor gymkhana, boxing, weight-lifting and a Mock Trial – the Hull (Dunmow) Flitch – to find a truly happy married couple. Arrangements for subsequent summers, especially 1935 and 1937, had a blueprint from which to work based on the 1933 experience. Fireworks rounded off these galas and all were eagerly attended. A format was there to be followed when there was need for entertainment in wartime.

Illuminations borrowed from Morecambe Corporation beautified City centre civic buildings, the Queens Gardens fountain spouted coloured jets, and plants in East Park were tastefully lit with suitable colours. Although I was not taken to see the fireworks on Coronation Day, I remember, as a great treat in 1937, being taken into the park, specially opened for the event in the evenings, and walking through the dark gardens. The sight of the illuminated rock gardens, in particular, stays in my memory, as the strange shapes of plants, seen in the cleverly-placed coloured lights, and the even stranger shadows of the newly-refurbished rockery made a novel and delightful picture that mild, dry evening.

* * *

Considerable change in the administration of the parks took place in the 1930s. Mr. H. B .Witty , Hull's second Parks Superintendent retired in 1929 after 44 years' service. His place was taken by Mr. George Henry Copley of Dewsbury, selected from 53 applicants and a short list of six. Mr. Witty, and Mr. Peak before him, had attended Committee meetings with a neat list of points constituting the Report and the matters were dealt with as they were read out. Mr. Copley was much more verbose and, after his first appearance at Committee, his reports were printed and circularised to the members before the meeting.

One of his early tasks was to consider the use and development of the Tower Grange estate. On 20 November 1929, just over a week after assuming his duties, he suggested that three of the Tower Grange glasshouses should house plants for civic functions and the rest be used for displaying plants of economic importance. The list of plants suggested is interesting: tea, coffee, cocoa, sugar, banana, eucalyptus, rubber, cotton, pineapple – and cocaine. British plants and those from temperate climates could be grown outside as there was a fair amount of ground in the newly-acquired estate. It would be a collection of educational value, he said. The Committee approved and Mr. Copley was to submit a scheme. By the middle of February 1930, he had bought a lot of tropical plants, planted rose beds in front outside and in July reported that cacti had been housed in a natural environment of rock and stones, all at Tower Grange.

However, at the 7 October 1930 meeting of the Parks and Burials Committee 'certain matters concerning the Parks Superintendent' were brought to light and on 30 October (after deliberation by a Sub-Committee) Mr.

Copley was severely reprimanded, his salary reduced by £100 p.a. and further increments of salary deferred for a year. On 13 November 1930, Mr. Copley gave three months' notice of his intention to quit his post, but on receiving this the Committee came down hard and said that either he leave at once or he would be dismissed. His misdemeanour was not revealed either in the minutes or the press, but there was such insistence afterwards of employees not taking other jobs while in Corporation service that I think Mr. Copley must have been doing a bit of 'consultancy' on the side.

Mr. Knight, the Pearson Park foreman, took over for the time being and in his first report said, 'With me, you will regret this unfortunate position that has occurred, but we shall have to make the best of it together…' On 17 December 1930, Mr. James Edward Roberts of Chesterfield was appointed Parks Superintendent. His priorities were different. Where Mr. Copley had bought exotics (including hot-house plants from Holderness House after Mr. Ferens' death that year), Mr. Roberts at once expressed surprise that there was no recognised nursery for plants in the City and regarded Tower Grange as a suitable site. For economy, for centralisation, and to provide bedding plants, trees and decorative plants for other parks, the streets and public functions, Tower Grange was an ideal place. This is how I remember the area. Mr. Copley's rose beds in front of the greenhouses behind the ornate fence with the concrete spheres on top of the brickwork and the cactus house remained. Only an L-shaped corridor of glasshouse was open to the public; the first section held seasonal displays of spring flowers or chrysanthemums, and around the corner were the curious and sometimes very beautiful cacti. Many people took this little detour as they walked along Holderness Road and it was a much appreciated amenity. The rest of the greenhouses held forced bulbs, bedding annuals, begonias, foliage plants and seasonal flowers to be used at appropriate times and places. Behind was a trapezoid plot where shrubs and trees were nurtured for planting and replacement in parks, open spaces and streets. Although, technically, the Tower Grange nurseries were a distinct entity, they seemed to be part of the park to everyone who used that entrance or viewed the displays.

The dual change of overall superintendence of the parks in the space of a year was obviously an upheaval, but as far as East Park was concerned, and Tower Grange in particular, the final outcome was advantageous.

In the early thirties many minutes recorded changes of status of employees and changes in wage structures. Economy was the order of the day as the national slump bit deep into people's lives. By the thirties, too, East Park was a large and complex concern, now nearly a mile long and a quarter of a mile wide, and containing diverse areas requiring a diverse or adaptable workforce. The Parks Superintendents had always been members of the City Engineer's staff and, as we have seen, the City Engineers had had very important roles in the development of East Park; there was far more to do than just gardening. In May 1934, the City Engineer asked to be relieved of all duties with respect to the control of the parks and cemeteries. A new administration was set up and the Parks, Allotments and Cemeteries Department as from

12 July 1934, its title usually abbreviated to the Parks Department. The Pearson Park Office of the General Superintendent (the new designation of the Parks Superintendent) was now inadequate and the new department took as its centre an office on the second floor of Ferensway Chambers. The change meant that its own staff would report on projects and approach the City Engineer as 'outsiders', thus separating quite clearly moneys expended by the City Engineers' and the Parks' Departments. Loans for major works would still need the sanction of the Ministry of Health under whose umbrella the administration of parks, open space and cemeteries continued to function as a matter of public health.

★ ★ ★

During the thirties, several major projects were mooted and some carried out. The Ferens Boating Lake, regularly a cause of expenditure because of leakage, needed a new concrete wall on the north side near the Pump House. The leaks were first reported in December 1932, and during the next year there was considerable outflow into the sewers behind rubble walls at the south-west end of the lake. As it would cost in the region of £1,200, Ministry sanction for a loan was needed and other lengths of the retaining wall were repaired or replaced at the same time. The Model Yacht Pond was also a drain on resources and over the years received treatment for leakage and cleaning that accounted for substantial sums of money. The Bowls Club constantly sought better accommodation, but, although plans and resolutions appeared to promise improvements from time to time, when it came to finance, deferment of each project was the order of the day. A late effort was the submission and acceptance of plans for a new Bowling Pavilion at the Tennis and Games Sub-Committee meeting of 7 July 1939, but the realisation was swallowed up in 'the present emergency', as the onset of war was so near.

Projects which would have made important changes to the shape and use of the park surfaced in committees and were never heard of again. In 1930, the Chief Librarian was hopeful of a new branch library for East Hull, to be built in East Park. Plans for this had been prepared as early as 1912, by Mr. J. H. Hirst, the then City Architect. A chosen site, of about 1,000 square yards, with a frontage of 120 feet on Holderness Road, was at the time part of a 'football playground', that is, the field between the lodge and East Park Avenue. In 1934, the Director of Museums attended a Parks and Burials Committee meeting where discussion ranged around the proposed museum in East Park and the Director described the type of exhibit to be housed there. The museum would also have been on Holderness Road, with access from the park and the road.

Neither project came to fruition. Money, of course, was a major barrier, but also there was, even before the war, a change coming over the ways in which people spent their leisure hours. Had the Woodford Centre been suggested at the time, one wonders if that would have had the go-ahead, whereas a museum and a library did not.

★ ★ ★

The Second World War

The outbreak of war in 1939 found the people of this country in some ways better prepared than in 1914. For one thing, the Great War was the first conflict for hundreds of years in which towns of mainland Britain were attacked. Hull had had its share of Zeppelin raids, and the inter-war increase in aviation meant the certainty of air-raids to come. In 1939-40 public air-raid shelters were built – long brick structures, with flat, reinforced concrete roofs – including three in East Park near the foreman's lodge. Certain excavations were made in some of the shrubberies as places where machinery could be hidden in case of the most dire scenario possible – invasion. Iron railings were taken in the belief that they could materially help the war effort; these included the railings and ornamental main gates on Holderness Road. Parts of the park were turned into allotments and there were demonstration plots to show people how to grow salads and vegetables in a small space. A barrage balloon was moored on the tennis courts behind The Willows and Corporation buses were parked at night on the carriageway under the trees.

The air raids came soon enough after the early months of uneasy calm – the 'phoney war' – and after Dunkirk they increased in number and ferocity. Tower Grange greenhouses were early casualties (April 1940) and the General Superintendent, in reporting the estimated cost of repairs (over £60) to the Parks and Burials Committee, said the greenhouses should be repaired as they contained many valuable plants, but, after that, all available glasshouse space had to be used for food production. The Corridor House at Tower Grange, through which many a housewife had strolled as a slight diversion from shopping, was closed to the public

The main avenue and conservatory between the wars.
Photograph courtesy of *Hull Daily Mail*.

at the end of the 1940 chrysanthemum season. The Superintendent did his best to secure deferment from war service for the workforce, declaring some of them to be 'market garden workers', but, even so, the park's staff, for gardening and otherwise, was severely depleted as the war went on.

The main conservatory had been closed on 11 January 1939 because of its dilapidated condition and I do not know if it re-opened, but on the night of 1/2 March 1941 it was shattered to such an extent that it was pulled down and the iron supports sold for scrap. About the same time, although instructions had been given for the re-glazing of one of the Tower Grange glasshouses, it was apparent that others would need complete reconstruction, so they were all to be left until after the war. Because of the lack of oars and of juvenile labour, the Ferens Boating Lake was used only during Bank Holiday weekends and ceased to be used completely for pleasure boating in the spring of 1944; by then only seven boats were serviceable. Chairs from around the bandstand were sent to Reception Centres of the Air Raid (Welfare) Committee, places where bombed-out people could go pending re-housing. Many clubs, which on the outbreak of war booked matches on the various park pitches and also on other recreation grounds in the City, had to cancel (a 'reasonable request' it was noted in the minutes of 13 December 1939), and the few friendlies that were played on these Corporation grounds were thereafter charged five shillings (25p) for the facility.

The grassy area of the park at the rear of James Reckitt Avenue became 30 allotments of varying sizes. Strict rules governed their use; for example, no livestock was allowed.

One tenant whose plot showed no evidence whatsoever of cultivation, but who was found to be keeping cockerels on his patch, had his tenancy terminated immediately. The mini-golf course, which was completed in April 1938 behind the Ings Road houses, was kept open until the spring of 1943, when it became too difficult to obtain new golf balls. Nineteen sheep at £4. 10s. each were then bought to graze the area, but I think it reverted to golf after the war, until about 1949 when finance for its provision was deleted from the estimates. Early in 1942, it seemed a good idea to keep pigs in the park, but the Superintendent said there was nowhere suitable, so a piggery was set up on Electricity Department land on Sutton House Road instead. Another scheme, to keep rabbits for food, was vetoed by the General Superintendent, as it would entail too much labour.

★ ★ ★

By 1941, it was obvious that the war was to continue for some time and the offer from O/C Hull Garrison of an athletics meeting and P.T. display open to Army units was welcomed as the nucleus of a summer entertainment in East Park. Bowls and tennis leagues were approached in order to organise tournaments in East and other parks, the preliminary rounds to be in East Park on 6 September, the date fixed for the East Park Gala. As a means of boosting morale it perhaps helped, but the weather, exceptionally bad on the day, did not. Not much publicity had been given to the event, but 2,044 adults and 1,587 children paid to get into the park for the Gala; the most successful part was the children's sports for which there were over 900 entries. The bowls tournament attracted 300 individual entries, but there were only ten couples on the tennis courts. The Tarran Waterloo Band entertained and £37. 17s. was handed over to the Air Raid Distress Fund.

This Gala was provided under the banner of 'Summer Holidays for the Workers' and, although the show was marred by miserable weather in 1941, great enthusiasm was shown in March 1942 when a Sub-Committee was formed to arrange the events for that summer's entertainment. 1942 had a brilliant summer and East Park and others in the City were venues for open-air drama by Miss H. M. Drasdo's well-known company and for various bands, including military bands, for concerts and the Police Dance Band for open-air dancing in East and West Parks. In East Park there were once again children's sports, as well as a Dig For Victory Show, bowls and tennis tournaments, a military sports meeting, a pet dog show, and the appearance of Sam Corry and his Performing Dog – a favourite the previous year. *Merrie England* was given by Miss Drasdo's company in both East and West Parks, tickets priced at 6d. and 3d. Twenty-five Cleethorpes donkeys provided rides for children. The Sub-Committee's minutes evoke the feeling of the time: of make-do-and-mend, of self-entertainment and of a general enthusiasm to do the best that circumstances allowed. It was during 1942 that the term 'Holidays at Home' was first used, a phrase that stuck in the language, with the realisation that holidays were permitted occasions, that workers had a right to them, even in wartime. It was, of course, a manufactured slogan, framed by people who had, before the war, regarded summer holidays as the norm.

The East Park Gala and other parks' activities were a financial success in 1942, but, come spring 1943, and the General Superintendent introduced a note of caution. The public was not responding as whole-heartedly as the Government wished to the idea of spending holidays at home. Hull people, he said, wanted holidays away from the present environment, somewhere with fewer air raids, and owners of swings and other funfair equipment were reluctant to bring their stock-in-trade into such a dangerous area. He also commented on the early termination of the bus service (the buses ceased to run at 9 p.m. and it was not until mid-October 1944 that they were allowed to run until 10 p.m.). The Superintendent deplored the exorbitant cost of out-of-town concert parties, noted the serious shortage of paper for publicity purposes, of indoor accommodation for concerts and dances, and of parks staff for duties beyond the norm, except for food production.

Nevertheless, 'Holidays at Home' were pursued in 1943 with renewed vigour and £2,000 was allowed in the estimates for 1944-5. Of the £2,000 provided for 1943, £1,762. 4s. 7d (£1,762.23p) was spent, with income of £1,629. 0s. 1d. Expenditure included £200 paid to an appointed organiser, a Hull man named Harry Hill. For 1944 his services were dispensed with, thereby saving £200 at a stroke.

In 1944, government circulars to local authorities were still urging provision, such as had been seen in the Hull parks, for holidays at home and, although there had been a lot of 'flu and similar ailments in its early months and the Committee knew many people would try to go away in the summer, some commitments had already been made by

March for entertainment in the parks. In May 1944, advertisements started to appear in the *Hull Daily Mail:* 'The Stay at Home Holiday Campaign'. Whit week offerings in East Park included 'The Gay Commanders' concert party and Elma Craft's Accordion Follies. On Whit Monday and Thursday there was dancing around the bandstand to the Hull City Police Dance Orchestra, and, throughout the week, children's boating, the water chute, a fun fair, roundabouts, swings, a mini-menagerie and pony rides would keep the children entertained. During the whole of the summer the Hull Bowls Effort proceeded: a series of matches, for which individual entrants paid a shilling; the profits, after National Savings Stamp prizes had been awarded, went to the Comforts for the Forces Fund. Various venues were used and East Park figured prominently.

East Park, a very large area, was not totally disturbed by these attractions. There were many places of peace and quiet and spaces for children to play, well away from the paid entertainments. In 1944, a gathering of Sunday School children sang hymns and there were fortnightly open air services for a few summers after that.

By the spring of 1945, the war was nearing its end, but eyes were on economy. 'Considering the appalling state of the City's finances . . .' is the start of one section of the minutes. £2,000 having been allocated for entertainments, it was hoped the revenue would reach this figure. The General Superintendent was very doubtful on this score, judging by 1944 when large sums had been paid for concert parties. He felt that such attractions as swings would be a better and less expensive substitute as they would give an assured income from the rentals. Cllr. R. E. Smith said it would turn the park into a funfair and nearby residents would not want that; he did not want 'a hurly-burly kind of entertainment'. But there had been funfairs (and some complaints) before, and with 'BERLIN A BURNING CITY OF DESOLATION' (*Hull Daily Mail* headline, 7 February 1944) and the end of hostilities in Europe clearly within grasp, some kind of summer festivity seemed appropriate – even though the local seaside resorts were also planning their own attractions in the hope of the easing of transport restrictions very soon.

However, the Park activities began to be referred to as 'The Summer Entertainments', which was felt by then to be more suitable than 'Holidays at Home', and Pickering and West Parks were more favoured venues than East Park. Cody's Circus, which had rented the King George V Playing Field in 1944, went to West Park in 1945 and East Park was the site for Poole's Caucasian Circus instead. Tommy Fisher's band and Elma Craft's Accordion Band played for open-air dancing on several evenings, but, as Government publicity was no longer urging people to take holidays at home and no longer suggesting that holidays at home were as good as holidays away from home, the enthusiasm for the kind of entertainment that had been popular in wartime seemed as though it might dwindle.

★ ★ ★

Signs of neglect were apparent in East Park as the war continued. The National Fire Service needed to be able to get water from the boating lake and the Parks and Burials

Committee reported on 12 July 1944 that the Fire Service was to install and take responsibility for certain items to ensure a supplementary water supply from the Foredyke and Lambwath Streams into the lake. During autumn 1944, part of the intake of the pump house and the lake were cleaned out and a number of cracks in the walls around the lake had been filled in. Also that autumn, the ladies' lavatories at the west end of the ornamental lake had been tidied up with pebble-dash outside, cement rendering inside, doors painted and the front flagged path replaced with concrete. The nearby children's lavatories, already closed for some time, were left as they were. Areas of excavation, dug at the outbreak of war to store machinery, were re-instated to their original form and in March 1945 the General Superintendent recommended that areas taken for food production should be returned to grass. Mr. Ogley, the East Park foreman, due to retire at the end of September, 1944, was re-engaged because of the manpower shortage. Woman power was in short supply, too, and the bowling greens had to close at 9 p.m. because there was insufficient female labour to keep them open until 10 o'clock. Not too surprisingly, nobody wanted to play bowls so late, even though the evenings were long and light during Double Summer Time.

★ ★ ★

On 13 June 1945, the Town Clerk reported a great increase of pilfering and vandalism in all the parks. Especially deplorable were the thefts of bedding plants, but there was also in East Park a particular problem: the removal of timber from the filter beds, diving platforms and buildings to make rafts for use on the Ferens Boating Lake. To some extent this was a measure of the popularity of boating and the disappointment of youngsters that the lake was not fully stocked with boats as some of them remembered or had been told by their elders. Elsewhere in the park, lavatory locks were constantly being broken off and cisterns filled with broken glass, so that the lavatories could not be kept in a sanitary condition.

The word 'vandalism' came into common currency in the language. As soon as repairs were effected, the damage started all over again. The Superintendent made several pleas for permission to try and get some fencing so that the park could be made secure and locked at night, but I remember that the type of chestnut fencing used after the war was in no way a deterrent to intruders and vandals.

As the war in Europe ended and the war in the Pacific still dragged on, people were eager to return, not just to a normality which they had known before the war, but to a different and freer way of life that some wartime experiences had shown to be possible. The Council had an immense task dealing with the ravaged City during a period when nationally the means were scarce and austerity the order of the day. The Parks Committee, in its sector of influence, was subject to the red tape, the scarcities and frustrations of the time, but tried heroically, perhaps even rashly, to give satisfaction to the people of Hull by dealing with as many aspects of their responsibility as they could in the shortest possible time.

'Getting back to normal'

The Foreman's house and office near Summergangs Road, completely destroyed by enemy action, was to be rebuilt, and from the Parks and Burials Committee meeting of 12 December 1945 came instructions to the City Architect to prepare plans and estimates. Buildings which had served as the Foreman's office and stores were in a bad state, but, as there were air raid shelters nearby, these were converted, the Home Office granting their transfer to the Corporation without charge. Subject to the planning approval normal for the times, one shelter became the Foreman's office and men's mess room, and the second and third were converted to a plant and tool house and a machinery store. The costs were relatively high because of the labour expended on the shelters' very solid construction. The lowest tender for rebuilding the house was £2,180. 9s. 2d. from C. H. Jaram of Cottingham, the cost to be reimbursed by the War Damage Commission.

The Council was about to improve Holderness Road from Summergangs corner to the City boundary. The Foreman's house was built and at once the rumours – which passed into local folklore – began. It was not in the right place! It had to be pulled down and rebuilt a bit further back! Time passed and the house still stood; Holderness Road was widened and the house still stood. The stories, of course, died away and eventually people forgot. However, the truth is found in the minutes of the Parks and Burials Committee for 9 March 1949. There had been consultation between the City Engineer's and the City Architect's staff, at which time the planning application was believed to be in order. The impending road widening had not been considered, and it was not realised until the house was built that its site was forward of the newly-required building line. It was resolved that 'the house must be set back to the new improvement line of Holderness Road as and when required'. This happened over half a century ago. I think the house will stay where it is.

★ ★ ★

At the other side of the main gates on Holderness Road, beyond the Park-keeper's lodge, was a First Aid Post. The status of this building had been discussed in July 1945, but it was left in the hands of the Health and Hospitals Sub-Committee for two years, after which time the situation was reviewed. But, when a deputation from the Parks Committee went to Matlock in the summer of 1946 to see the only portable dance hall in the country, they decided to hire it for East Park from the proprietor, John Collins, who was to receive 60% of the takings, subject to a guarantee of £100 per week. The dance hall, a marquee with suitable flooring, was erected on land fronting Holderness Road and the old First Aid Post was then converted for use as an annexe and crush room. The dance hall was initially hired from 5 to 28 September 1946, but the period was extended into October, by which time negotiations were under way to buy the hall; it would be stored in the First Aid Post in winter. A firm decision to buy came on 12 March 1947: the price was £1,750 and the hall was to be in use not later than 1 May 1947. The Parks Committee took over the First Aid Post on 10 December 1947 and applications were made both for a Music, Singing and Dancing Licence and for permission to heat it. It was then converted into a permanent Dance Hall using the portable floor from the marquee; an opening party and dance was held on New Year's Eve to herald 1948.

East Park Ballroom became a popular East Hull venue, open three nights a week:

Tuesdays	Olde Time Night	8-11 p.m.	2s.(10p)
Fridays	Popular Night	8-12 p.m.	2s.
Saturdays	Modern Night	7.30-11.30 p.m.	2s. 6d. (12½p)

– the remaining nights left available for whist drives, concerts or private functions. Charges for hiring the hall seem absurdly low to us today, but, as wages in Hull were not matching the soaring prices for many goods and especially for services, the hall for, say, a wedding reception meant for many the outlay of a week's wages. In modern terms, the use of the hall up to 11 p.m. cost £3.50, with £1 charge for each additional hour. The piano cost 50p to hire and the amplifying equipment 75p. Tommy Fisher took the ballroom on a regular basis for a long time after the war and dancing to his band on a Saturday night was a very popular pastime.

★ ★ ★

With the retirement of Mr. Roberts as Superintendent, came a departure from past procedure, because the Council sought a person whose main qualification was in administration rather than in horticulture. The man chosen was Mr. Barry Roscoe, who took up the appointment on 1 January 1947.

A great deal of necessary work was carried out after the war, despite restrictions and risen prices. Essential repairs and reconstruction at Tower Grange were done, and by autumn 1946 a quarter of the heated greenhouse space was allowed to be used for non-edible plants. The Town Clerk applied to the Ministry of Fuel and Power for half the space to be used for propagation and related functions, but so dire was the situation in the mid- to late forties that this was not permitted.

The lake was cleaned out, the islands reconstructed to some extent, and estimates for a new boat house obtained from the City Engineer. New boats were purchased and old ones repaired, certain changes were made at the landing-stages as portable pontoons were bought for use as jetties ; floating beams divided the huge lake into sections. The southern ornamental pond was also cleaned out in the autumn of 1949 and, once drained, the water was not replaced. I think the other, smaller ornamental lake had lost much of its water during the war and may also have been drained at the same time. The East Park Open Air Theatre opened on Thursday evening, 22 June 1950, with a performance of *The Merry Wives of Windsor* by Miss Drasdo's company. I have been told that the theatre was in a bowl formed by the larger drained pond, but have no recollection of it, nor of how long it continued to function.

In September 1950, the most advantageous tender for the dilapidated bandstands of both East and Pearson Parks was accepted and C. A. Hill & Co. of Hull paid £150 for features that had been the focus of much pleasure. The bandstands had become obsolete, it was said, because of the popularity of concert parties and other types of entertainment provided in recent years. Nevertheless, the area was to be asphalted for open-air dancing, which continued with piped music. Five years later, it was proposed to construct a roller-skating rink where the bandstand had been in East Park. Whether or not people skated on the 'dancing floor' asphalt, I'm not sure, but it is likely that, once put forward as an idea, the general public would turn it into a *fait accompli*. In May 1960, application to the Parks Committee for a roller-skating rink in West Hull was met with the comment that the Committee would wait until facilities were provided in East Hull and observe how they fared before considering a similar area in the western part of the City. Later, in 1963, a picture in the *Hull Daily Mail* shows a rock garden nearing completion with the caption, 'A new look in East Park where a lawn and rock garden . . . replaces the old bandstand.' Not a skating rink.

* * *

The long-awaited finale to a series of requests and deferments came when the East Park Veterans' Bowling and Recreation Club Pavilion on Holderness Road was officially handed over on 10 November 1959. It provided a brick-built clubhouse with reasonable amenities for meeting and social activities. The architecture is of the rectangular-box variety typical of post-war austerity, but continues to be a useful venue for the Veterans to the present time.

* * *

One of the park's oldest features, the ornamental gates and fence, had been taken for salvage at the onset of war. Moves to replace them did not have priority, but in 1951 the General

Superintendent produced a sketch plan of a new entrance which was approved in principle. This matter surfaced again in 1961; then in November, 1963, when the Superintendent offered a new plan, costing £5,200, it too was approved in principle, rescinding previous schemes. So the controversial new main entrance to East Park came into being in July 1964. The ornamental cavity block walls were the object of public scorn (comments were heard on the bus, loud and clear, as one passed the park!) as being unworthy successors to their Victorian counterparts. Apart from criticism of the pillars' design of geometrical shapes on concrete blocks, there was a general feeling that they were shoddy and would be vandalised and crumbling in a year or two. The gates themselves are vertical bars without decoration and the whole entrance is quite typical of the Spartan design of the early 1960s. I am now used to them, but each time I pass am reminded of textile designs of the same period, of geometrical shapes set in not-quite-symmetrical patterns, which many people then had in their homes. Much of what was built in the 1960s has already gone; East Park entrance has stood the test of nearly forty years.

East Park Veterans' Bowling and Recreation Club Pavilion of 1959, still in use, 2001.

Into Modern Times

Quite apart from new projects, there was plenty to be done in the park. A new ticket office, incorporating a messroom, for the staff, was built near the boating lake, itself a constant focus for work. Anglers were allowed to re-stock the lake with fish and ticket prices for fishing in the lake fixed at 6d. and 3d. for adults and children respectively, while a season ticket cost 3s. (15p). The appearance of a lot of dead fish in the lake in the late summer of 1956 stopped all angling for a while. The problem stemmed from the old difficulty of the lake's water supply and the impossibility of preventing leakage. The Hull and East Yorkshire River Board and the City Analyst were consulted and a meeting with the East Yorkshire Fisheries Consultative Association discussed fishing policy.

In early 1957, the Superintendent reported on the cost of disposal of outlet water and the extra pumping needed to replace water in the lake. A further supply from the Foredyke Stream would bring in undesirable seeds of weeds which would incur more cost to keep down: a necessary operation, so that boats, especially motor boats, could move freely. Sealing against leakage was again carried out, but fishing was not allowed. Consultation was still going on in 1959, and the matter of the lake's water supply again under discussion in January 1963, as the Lambwath Stream was shortly to be filled in. Discussions with outside bodies to improve the lake as a fishery were fruitless until the problem of water supply was satisfactorily solved.

Fishing must have resumed some time in the late 1950s

as the Hull and East Riding Wildfowlers' conservation section asked the Committee to prohibit fishing lines and hooks because of the recent number of injuries to wildfowl on the lake. The Parks Committee responded by resolving that fishing should be prohibited. That was on 21 July 1965. This situation continued despite protestations from the Anglers' Association and the East Riding Association of Youth Clubs. People defied the ban and, I suppose, partly on the principle of 'if you can't beat 'em, join 'em', the prohibition was removed in September 1969. There were conditions. The lake was not to be restocked, no 'spinners' were to be used and the rods had to be of an approved type. There would be a review at the end of the first season. The Amalgamated Anglers tried for a concession by asking, if the Association paid a £20 cover for the season, could its members be allowed to fish gratis? It wasn't granted, but fishing continued amicably enough under the 1969 terms.

The Wildfowlers had a reserve for rearing mallard and other species which they ringed and released in various East Riding waterways. This organisation was responsible for the introduction of a nucleus of greylag and Canada geese to East Park in 1961. Some of their descendants were taken to Hornsea Mere. The other geese seen in the park are pink-footed and now seem to predominate, though there may be a seasonal fluctuation. The proliferation of wild geese was perhaps even more abundant than the Wildfowlers foresaw, and to some people the presence of these strong, demanding birds is intimidating to say the least, and they do make a mess, especially near the lake at Hawkesbury Street.

The lake's problems did not go away, nor could they, as it

Fishing in the boating lake in July 1995: the final of the junior match organised by officers of the Bransholme Police Station.
Photograph courtesy of *Hull Daily Mail.*

Canada geese and mallard predominate in a crowd of hungry wild fowl: a winter scene.
Photograph courtesy of *Hull Daily Mail.*

is a large stretch of 'living' water, not a sterile tank. It has to be cleaned periodically and on one such occasion people in James Reckitt Avenue collected signatures on a petition. It was mid-May 1984, and one can imagine the reaction of nearby house-holders to the piles of drying mud and slime on the lakeside as summer approached. By that time control of the park was in the hands of the Leisure Services Committee and the Director responded to the petition by describing what had been done to enhance the park at the back of James Reckitt Avenue by the replacement of certain old trees. He also reassured the petitioners (one hopes) by referring to tests for various bacteria in the mud, all of which had proved negative. The mud was allowed to dry before it was carted away, but certainly in this case removal was hastened by the petition.

★ ★ ★

A preliminary report for a new nursery garden and greenhouses on Longhill appeared in March 1957. This would spell redundancy for the Tower Grange complex. The East Hull main drainage drove through that area two years later and Tower Grange was becoming distinctly run-down. When in 1963 a letter was received from the Chief Constable asking for the Council to consider police acquisition of part of the site for a new Divisional H.Q., this was agreed. Tower Grange Police Station became operational on 1 April 1974 and was formally opened on 6 December that year by the Rt. Hon. Roy Jenkins, M.P, Secretary of State for the Home Department. Beyond the Police Station are Corporation bungalows for elderly persons, some built on the open ground that was used to nurture shrubs

and trees for the streets and roads of the City. Their address derives from the fact that Ald. C. J. Hurley was Chairman of the Housing Committee in 1963.

The new Longhill Nursery was in progress long before the Tower Grange area was fully built upon. In its early days came the Arctic winter of January-March 1963 when a large number of trees and shrubs were destroyed by the severe frost. Then, in March, when spring should have been showing its signs, the Hunsley Beacon Beagles were called in to chase out (not to hunt) the many starving hares which invaded the nursery and gained some sustenance by stripping the barks of the hundreds of young saplings.

★ ★ ★

Through whatever rose-tinted lenses ladies of my acquaintance gaze back to scenes of youthful times in East Park, one item is usually remembered with revulsion: the drinking cup at the play area. There was an outside tap with a metal cup attached by a chain. Fastidious children wiped the metal cup's side carefully; the most fastidious went away without drinking. Adverse reports on the arrangement came from the Medical Officer of Health and the City Analyst, but the Committee merely replaced the existing cup with one of similar material, smooth inside and with a plain top, not seeing 'any reason to make any change in the type of cup already in use'. This was in 1936, a time when new schools were being equipped with hygienic drinking fountains. At that time the old Gothic drinking fountain still stood at the confluence of the park's entrance and the encircling carriage drive.

However, reports soon after the war, from the Ministry of Health, the City Analyst and the Water Engineer declaring the swimming ponds to be both inadequate and insanitary, *were* heeded, and an earlier idea of converting them into an open-air lido was looked upon as a possibility. In any case, the ponds were closed at the end of the 1949 season, not to re-open, for health reasons.

The 'baby boom' of the immediate post-war years meant that by 1949-50 there were more children using the paddling pool and, as a consequence, more accidents. The death in the bathing pool of a nine-year-old boy was another factor prompting reconsideration of the use of the bathing pools; lesser, but still alarming, accidents at the paddling pool led to the construction of a tubular metal and chain-link fence at the boating lake side of the pool to keep youngsters away from the big lake. Nevertheless, after the bathing ponds' closure, it was impossible to keep children from bathing in the boating lake during hot weather, so immediate moves were made towards the provision of better bathing facilities. Visits were made to Ilkley and Nelson to see their open-air pools, and plans and photos of pools in many different places were studied; but the time was not ripe for a major project. The East Park Lido was not formally considered again for many years, even though it had been said in Committee that construction of an open-air lido should begin in Festival of Britain year (1951) with a view to early completion.

The old gothic drinking fountain within the park's main entrance. This picture may be just before the Second World War.
Photograph courtesy of Flashpoint Supplement, *Hull Daily Mail*, September 1997.

The Lido, June 1978.
Photograph courtesy of *Hull Daily Mail*.

Other local firms were involved: Abba's, the plumbers, and Kirkby, electricians. The pool measured 132 feet by 48 feet and depths varied between 3 feet and 5 feet 6 inches. The changing and clothes storage area occupied more than 5,800 square feet, including 94 light blue and white glazed brick cubicles divided equally between males and females. A board fence on the north and eastern sides made a necessary windbreak and there remain many happy pictures of swimmers and sunbathers in the open air in the 1960s and 1970s. The water was heated on an off-peak electricity tariff.

Some of the buildings housing the essential works were let into the ground to a depth of about six feet and this resulted in difficulties of construction and maintenance as the ground thereabout was pretty waterlogged. Even with tracked earth-moving equipment it had been hard to shift the spongy crust of earth. The total cost was about £100,000, a far cry from the cheap Guardians' labour that had constructed the old swimming ponds. The lido, completed six weeks ahead of schedule, was opened on 18 July 1964 by Cllr. A. Parker, Chairman of the Baths Committee.

There followed years of use and enjoyment, but global

By 1960, with post-war reconstruction and repairs (almost) done, the lido became more than a possibility. Together, the City Engineer and General Superintendent indicated a layout from which the consulting engineering firm of Pick, Everard, Keay and Gimson of Leicester produced the final working plan. Tenders in the spring of 1963 brought the actual construction to a local firm, Stepney Contractors, Ltd., and, as the following winter was mild, work progressed well, so the lido pool was ready to be tested by Easter 1964. Then building work began on the housing for pumps, boilers, filter and chlorination plants and, of course, for changing rooms.

The remodelled paddling pool and play area, 1984.
Photograph courtesy of *Hull Daily Mail*.

A shallow basin where the swimming ponds once were, September 2001.

warming did not always reach this part of the east coast and when, after years of deliberation, the Ennerdale Centre was opened, the East Hull Baths refurbished, and the Woodford Centre built in the park itself, the public gradually moved back to indoor swimming. The Lido had technical problems, too, and, following years of decline, was closed down and then demolished in 1988.

The nearby children's playground was remodelled in the mid-1970s and then, after demolition of the Lido, the area made into a more extensive playground, latterly surrounded with strong fencing. The paddling pool was more than filled in; it is now a great grassy mound overlooking the lake. The old swimming ponds now form a tree-fringed shallow basin of surprisingly wide extent.

★ ★ ★

The Woodford Centre's origins go back at least to the early 1960s. The way to its realisation was very rough and long. On 29 June 1961 members of the Parks Committee attended a Planning Sub-Committee meeting at which outline application for an indoor sports hall in East Park was discussed. After agreement in principle, with possible modification to include rifle shooting, and then approval by the Sports Council, the time moved on to the mid-sixties, but unfortunately the start of 1967 also heralded a Government Period of Severe Restraint and the Ministry of Housing and Local Government refused loan consent.

In January 1968, local authorities were asked to review all capital expenditure, deferring anything beyond housing and schools that was not essential. The project was still on the table ; when the North Eastern Gas Board asked if a mains pipe could be driven through the park, crossing the site earmarked for the Sports Hall, an urgent but amicable discussion led to a decision to take the pipe by another route, leaving the Sports Hall site free. The City's finances at the time were in a pretty poor state and unable to cope with this major project, even though the Ministry had by then sanctioned it via the Sports Council. In fact, it had been graded a Category A project to be started as soon as possible. That was 22 January 1969.

Eventually, at 9 a.m. on Good Friday, 9 April 1982, Phase I of the Sports Centre was opened to the public. The early demand for casual bookings was higher than expected, but they were carefully recorded to ascertain which activities interested people the most. Courses were soon established across a wide age and activity range, including Badminton, fencing, football, Karate and Judo (for which latter Karen Briggs, the Judo champion, was one of the coaches). A weight-conditioning course of basic exercises led to a certificate giving the holder access to casual sessions in the sophisticated weight-training room.

The formal opening, by John Prescott, M.P., was on 27 April 1982 and speeches were also given by the Lord Mayor, (Cllr. Mrs. Phyllis Clarke), Cllr. Mrs. Mima Bell and Cllr. Harry Woodford, after whom the Centre was named. It was a time when the Council was having great sport with names and notices – boards seemed to be popping up everywhere – and I wish I had written down the different names which appeared outside the Sports Hall, before the 'Woodford Centre' was fixed upon. It is a fitting name as Cllr. Woodford has great interest in East Hull and long association with the Parks Committee.

Phase II included a leisure pool and the *Civic News* of January/February 1968 promised 'A Tropical Paradise down Holderness Road' in the spring. Reference was made to a 'lagoon-shaped' pool complete with palm trees, beach and wave machine. Tropical paradises don't usually smell of chlorine, but, that aside, it's a nice leisure pool, enjoyed by all ages for fun, though not for serious swimming. Phase II quadrupled the Centre's size and added accommodation for serious sports activity as well as the fun pool. Phase II opened in June 1986, and is well attended, judging by the number of cars in the quite ample car park on Holderness Road.

★ ★ ★

When Mr. Roscoe retired in May 1963, the *Mail* headline, 'Mr. Greenfingers will take it easy in his City of Flowers,' led a long column describing his 16-year tenure of the post of General Superintendent. Coming to Hull when wartime neglect was only too apparent, he did much to brighten up the city by bringing flowers into the streets for all to see every day. His previous post was in Halifax where he had designed the country's first electrically-heated central nursery and thus was very able to take over the embryonic Longhill nursery. His idea of a park was more open than the Victorians' and he abolished 'Keep off the Grass' signs, a move that I think went too far. His place was taken by his Deputy, Mr. J. A. Milne, and it was he who created the new gardens below the terrace in East Park.

The terrace beyond the old conservatory was approached by flights of steps between rose-beds below the retaining wall. From childhood, I remember neatly-raked paths of cream-coloured chippings and the less-than-beautiful boiler house behind the conservatory. Once on the terrace, although only a few feet above the main avenue, a vista was afforded of the major flower-beds and floral clock beyond. The top of the terrace wall was covered with climbing roses, some with tiny pink flowers, others of the American pillar variety.

The gardens below the terrace were radically altered in 1968. With no conservatory in front, there was plenty of space, and a modern geometrical garden of sunken areas and raised beds was made, giving sheltered places for seats below the level of the main path. At first, the shrubs were small and annual planting was possible between them ; the garden, although sheltered, was sunny and friendly. As everything grew, the general air soon changed, because many of the shrubs were dark-leaved or evergreen varieties which overshadowed the whole aspect and left little room for under-planting. Small trees on or near the terrace were also allowed to grow. The open promenade that the terrace used to be, with a few nicely-placed standard rose trees with metal 'crinolines' to train the strands of small roses, has become enclosed and gloomy and somewhat mossy underfoot.

The main avenue was always bordered with low privet hedges, so the flower beds were admired from a little distance and the viewer had the whole vista in a single picture. There were little gaps in the hedges for the gardeners, but the planted areas behind were sacrosanct and the general public acted as willing vigilantes if small boys nipped through the gaps to play hide-and-seek inside the hedges. The mound

'Completed section of the new ornamental
garden, East Park', 6 February 1970.
Photograph courtesy of Hull Daily Mail.

The same garden, September 2001, showing its
overgrown state.

behind became more and more covered in foliage, evergreens and silver birch predominating, and now is a very solid backdrop, the trees completely obscuring the shape of 'Monkey Hill' and covering any vestige of the old 1920s maze.

The floral clock fell into disrepair but remained throughout the 1960s, I believe. Mrs. Maisie Parkes offered a new one as a personal gift to the park, in appreciation of the support given by the people of Hull for her charity functions. After some negotiations, for some reason, this offer came to nothing. However, a clock was reinstated where it ever had been, as a 'timely' reminder of the 700th anniversary of Kingston upon Hull's charter. Instead of Pott's clockwork mechanism, the new clock worked by electricity, the manufacturers being Smith's of Derby. The Lord Mayor, Cllr. Brian Petch, unveiled the new clock on Sunday, 4 April 1999, with a small ceremony. I intended to take a photo soon after, but a friend told me it was badly vandalised within a week of the opening. Now it is in a sorry state of disrepair above ground, as the areas behind the privet hedges are no longer sacrosanct as they used to be.

★ ★ ★

At the end of the terrace is the aviary. Over the years it has been altered and extended, so that now its total area is nearly twice the original. In recent years the wire covering has been strengthened and there is, in consequence, not such a clear view of the birds. It is still a fine aviary and the birds are well-kept. A further cage was added for larger birds, and there were peacocks at one time. There were also macaws,

and so mischievous and destructive are these beautiful birds that foliage plants or small trees in the cage would have been ripped to nothing very quickly. To brighten up the otherwise drab enclosure the end wall was painted with a lively mural. As macaws were housed there, it was almost a case of gilding the lily. One feature that I remember from the mid-thirties was the slope leading up to the aviary level from the terrace, an adjunct to the original steps. Slopes were made in other places in the park at that time, in the rockery, for example, so that mothers with prams or people pushing wheelchairs could walk easily to see the park's beauties.

★ ★ ★

A long letter to the *Hull Daily Mail* as far back as 28 October 1901 from one signing himself 'Hullite' included a suggestion for a wild animal enclosure in the park to encourage tourists. It would cost 'but a small bagatelle,' he said, 'now that the parks are paid for'. Think not of gentle deer and wallabies: Hullite recommended that there should be lions and tigers, a small zoo, in fact, but the first animals that I know were kept in the park were St. Kilda sheep. A mention is made of them in a minute of 16 May 1935, as a dog had attacked one.

The ornamental lakes had been joined by a rather dark stretch of water behind the 'heights' of Khyber Pass. This was drained when the ornamental lakes were no more. There may have been some water remaining, but the area, on the main carriage drive, was dank and well overshadowed for much of the day. This was opened up, extended and made into an animal enclosure in the early 1960s and a deer house built there in 1966. It was an area which seemed to be bedevilled by vandalism, so frequent (it seemed to me) were the press reports on the subject. There were Sika deer, wallabies, rabbits and guinea pigs in the compound; perhaps Hullite's lions and tigers would have deterred the intruders. I think there were also fallow deer and llamas. In 1966, when some wallabies were introduced from the Sewerby stock, one of them died and had to be replaced quite soon. Wallabies were favourites when they had young as it was a curiosity to see the joey peeping out of the mother's pouch. About the same time, a few Jacob's sheep were bought: a ram, three ewes and a lamb.

During 2001, an enemy even worse than mindless vandals has threatened the animal enclosure: foot-and-mouth disease. When the scourge was first discovered, in February, and livestock owners all over the country began to take precautions, all the south-western end of the park was sealed off. That was, in effect, the original park. Disinfectant pads were laid at the entrances and very few people went in for some months. Then, because the disease did not strike this part of Yorkshire, a huge enclosure, a kind of *cordon sanitaire*, was made around the original animal compound, and people were allowed into the rest of the park. I walked through the park one glorious September morning recently. To see

'wild' animals grazing in dappled sunshine in the distance of this new enclosure was a much more natural view than of animals seen at close quarters in conventional zoos, however well-kept.

The watch-tower has, of course, gone, but Khyber Pass, now within the enlarged enclosure, is barely visible. It is surprising what one season can do, but I think some of this growth is of longer duration than the foot-and-mouth outbreak. The children's adventure playground created after 1965 when the bridge over Khyber Pass was demolished and the Arab doors removed would be even greater 'magic' (as one man described the playground to me) now than

Jacob's sheep in the 1960s.
Photograph courtesy of *Hull Daily Mail.*

before, though the animal enclosure is strictly forbidden to all but the staff nowadays. A fairly narrow strip at the outer edge is reserved for fancy poultry, white geese and peacocks. Some of the peacocks were lazing and preening in the sun, but one had leapt the fence and was keeping company with a couple of pink-footed geese on the path, much to the screaming delight or consternation of a small girl taking a walk with her father.

★ ★ ★

Far from dwindling down to nothing, shows in the park have taken modern tastes on board and continue to flourish. They have become less like village shows and much more like trade fairs. The last one I visited, in August 2001, occupied a very big part of the original park abutting Summergangs Road and included a funfair, fast food stalls, trade and charity stalls, a gymnastics display, a display by the Army, vintage cars and other attractions. There was a produce show in one marquee, but, although the exhibits were to be commended, their numbers were pathetic in comparison with the first decades after the war. This was a major change from the earlier shows : less local individual input. Thousands of people were there, a good-natured crowd for many of whom it was a good afternoon of free entertainment. The park is also the venue for pop music concerts and the like, culminating, if that is the right word, in this year's 'Feel the Noise' extravaganza. The very title makes me cringe, but perhaps the people who

Behind the wire which extends the animal enclosure is the site of the old watchtower. Unseen is Khyber Pass, now inaccessible. September 2001.

Hull Show, August 2001.
Photograph courtesy of Miss W. Rawdon

gained great enjoyment from this highly successful show would not be the least interested in visiting a marquee filled with good local garden produce. There are complaints, of course, as there have been from the 1920s onwards. Chiefly the complaints are about excessive noise, but of recent years more disturbing descriptions of people's anti-social behaviour at the 'gigs' and their defilement of neighbouring gardens have appeared in the press.

I recognise that the park is there for the needs and enjoyment of the people of Hull as those change with time. In 1948, what was intended to be an influential report was commissioned by the Council from E. Prentice Mawson, and although, like the Abercrombie Report, it was not followed up, it did contain this wise comment: that the park should be a place serving many purposes and '. . . in which the young may play and the old may rest, *without either becoming an annoyance to the other'*. The 'young' play differently now and the 'old' of 1948 are very active in ways undreamed of then, but the point is made that the park should serve many purposes and a wide range of people, amicably.

What with Hull's 700th anniversary and the Millennium hard upon it, a number of projects were started or came to fruition. In April 1999, the gates from the former R.A.F. station on Wawne Road were restored at a cost of £3,000 and brought to East Park to form the roadway gate on James Reckitt Avenue opposite Gillshill Road. It was a nice little ceremony with some young Air Corps members, R.A.F. personnel and veterans there to see the Lord Mayor, Cllr. Brian Petch, cut the ribbon. Mr. Len Bacon, instigator of the scheme to save the gates and use them at the park, was also present. The gates have been furnished with the three crowns of Hull and a sensible non-destructible plaque, giving a brief account of their history and provide a firm gate for that entrance to the park.

About this time, a high, elegant, metal fence was put up on James Reckitt Avenue opposite Malet Lambert School. Provided with a gate between brick pillars, it, too, secures this side of the park and keeps the geese from wandering on to the road o' nights ! Its counterpart sealed off the Hawkesbury Street edge of the lake .

In 1998, a consultancy firm, Land Design Associates, was called in to advise the City Council on the best way to utilise the park. That it had become shabby there is no doubt. The park is used more roughly than in its early days and there is lack of care from some of its visitors: children who roam indiscriminately, adults who let children behave without much restraint, children and adults who leave litter, children and youths who break down shrubs and branches in making their ways through shrubberies instead of using the paths and downright vandals determined to damage, injure or steal.

High Hopes

To restore the park will cost a great deal of money. One source for such projects is the Heritage Lottery Fund. In preparation for a bid for a grant from this fund, in the year 2000, the eastern end of the lake was sealed off with a clay dam at the bridge, the fish removed and the water pumped from one side of the dam to the other. Coarse fish, roach, carp, bream, tench and pike, were transferred to the south-western section of the lake. Clearing out silt and rubbish, sealing leaks, tidying up the islands and strengthening the lake edges were all done in this long operation.

In the spring of 2001, English Heritage designated East Park as Grade II on its list of Parks and Gardens of Historic Interest, a listing which means that the City Council must inform English Heritage of any contemplated changes. As the Council put in a bid the previous year for Heritage Lottery funding, which was confirmed subject to approval of the proposed plan, there are hopes that money will be available for all the major work that is sorely wanting. The decision is expected in June 2002.

★ ★ ★

It was my intention in writing the park's story to show what a complex, diverse, expensive, but worthwhile enterprise it is. It is not my intention to give a personal opinion of what should be done, except in one particular. At the Parks Presentation evening in early 2000, at which strategies for the development of Hull's parks in the 21st century were outlined and discussed, one of the first comments from a member of the public was, in effect, that all the plans would be of no avail unless the parks were secure and patrolled. This evoked spontaneous applause from the public audience, myself included.

East Park owes its existence to far-sighted Victorians, but it is not a relic nor an Ancient Monument. It should be a place to be enjoyed by people of all ages, with respect and in safety.